ENGLISH OBSERVED

Richard MacAndrew

Acknowledgements

My thanks go to Sheila Borges, Editor of Practical English Teaching, who was interested enough to publish the articles which inspired this book; to Michael Lewis for his help and encouragement during the past eighteen months, and for providing inspiration when it was most needed; to Jimmie Hill for his thoughtful and useful suggestions; and to Cathy Lawday for helping to collect a lot of the data, reading the manuscript, providing valuable comments, and looking after the boys.

The chapters on comparatives, conditionals, prepositions and the apostrophe are all based on articles which appeared in Practical English Teaching; and, with the exception of conditionals, have also appeared as poster presentations at IATEFL conferences.

We are grateful to Noel Watson for drawing the cartoons; to 'Private Eye' for permission to reproduce the cartoon on page 16, and to Nigel Ellis for help with the artwork.

EDITOR'S INTRODUCTION

Every native speaker is used to being asked 'Can you say . . . . ?' They all know, too that your questioner will be happy with either a decisive 'Yes' or a decisive 'No'. The route to unpopularity is to reply 'Well, it's difficult to say . . . It depends on the context . . . I've never heard/seen it myself but it's definitely possible'. For many learners and teachers black and white answers are fine, but grey is an unpopular colour!

In this book the author tackles the issues of 'right' and 'wrong' language, attitudes to 'correctness', the strengths and weaknesses of reference books and a host of associated topics. He writes from the perspective of a working teacher who has thought his own way through many of these issues. He invites the reader to think about some of the difficulties and questions which have worried him as he has tried to answer students' questions, prepare them for examinations, deal with extraordinary 'rules' which students have learned elsewhere, etc. etc. Serving teachers will recognise many of the dilemmas the reader is invited to think about.

The book will help any teacher, alone, or in a small group, on pre-service or in-service teachers' courses, to focus on, and think more clearly about, many of the issues which trouble teachers on a day-to-day basis. The author does not impose his own answers, but encourages useful questioning by the readers.

The final chapter will provide scope for discussion for many non-native teachers and students, at both school and university. The collection of unusual examples, collected over a very short period of time, and all authentic native-speaker English, should both shock and stimulate those who think the English of language textbooks, or even reference books, is 'the real thing'. The real language, used by native speakers, is richer and more varied than is often thought. The author encourages 'open eyes, open ears, and an open mind'. His book represents a stimulus to all who are curious about English and how it is taught.

Michael Lewis   Hove, 1991

CONTENTS

Introduction 1

Part One - Background 7
1. Language Awareness 8
2. Grammars 11
3. Influences 15

Part Two - Data 19
4. Comparatives 20
5. Prepositions 24
6. The Simple Past 30
7. Adverbs 34
8. Conditional Sentences 37
9. The Apostrophe 44
10. Word Order 50
11. Gerund or Infinitive? 54
12. Number 56
13. Other Possible Changes 60

Part Three - Implications 65
14. Acceptability 66
15. Language Change 71
16. Inventing New Language 75
17. The Power of Language 79
18. Implications for Language Teachers 83
19. Reference Books 89
20. Data Collection 92
21. Examples for Discussion 96
22. Postscript 102
Bibliography 104

INTRODUCTION

Have you ever found yourself disagreeing with a language point in your coursebook? Have you ever looked something up in a grammar and been dissatisfied with the explanation given? Have you ever heard a native speaker say something that you might correct if one of your students said it? If any of these apply to you, then you might be interested in some of the observations that follow.

This is not a conventional grammar book; nor is it intended to be. The basis of the book is the collection of authentic language - sayings and writings of native speakers - that I have built up over the last few years. Many of the authentic items I have collected would be condemned by language teachers and grammarians. However, they are all examples of what native speakers of English have actually said or written and raise questions for anyone interested in English and how it is taught. They range from the quite extraordinary:

to the strange but correct:

'Her father lighted a Gaulois'

to the commonplace but universally reviled:

PROPERTIE'S
WANTED

I will look at the utterances, grouping them in a reasonably systematic fashion, and at the same time raise a number of questions which I feel are important for grammarians and language teachers and, indeed, for anyone who is interested in how English is really used by a wide range of native speakers.

The real beginning of this book was in 1975 when a totally untrained graduate was just beginning a career as a teacher of English as a foreign language (EFL). This was before the days of formal teacher training in the field. At best, in those days, a one-week training course was offered in Britain before taking up a post abroad. In such a state of ignorance, a great reliance was obviously placed on the coursebook. The book I first used contained some fairly typical grammatical explanations, including one on comparatives. It also contained - at different points in the book - two differing examples of comparatives - on one page *commoner* and on another *more common*. This initially aroused my curiosity and led to many observations of native speakers 'breaking' the so-called grammatical rules of the formation of comparative adjectives. *More fast* and *more easy* proved more common (commoner) than one might expect from the textbook rules - see Chapter 4 on comparatives.

This led to the observation that there were other 'rules' that seemed to be ignored or broken fairly regularly. Eventually, after many years of observing these strange linguistic phenomena I started to record them and draw some tentative conclusions.

The next major source of encouragement came about in a rather odd way. In a book review for Practical English

Teaching (June 1987) of Michael Lewis's 'The English Verb', I wrote:

> 'The assertion that *"How are you spelling Lewis?"* is a possible though unusual sentence I find extraordinary. It may be possible in his circles but no-one I know has ever come across it.'

'How are you spelling Lewis?'

In a later letter to PET (December 1987) regarding the same review I dug the hole a bit deeper:

> 'My own name ... is subject to a variety of spellings and yet I cannot recall a single occasion when anyone has asked me how I am spelling it.'

Fortunately, I never claimed that the phrase in question was actually 'wrong' - only 'extraordinary'. Since that time, I have come across the expression a number of times, even from members of my own family !

The whole incident highlighted an important consideration for everyone involved in language teaching. We must be open in more ways than one: we must keep our eyes and our ears open to the language that is around us; and we must keep our minds open to the evidence that we are confronted with - however unexpected that evidence may sometimes appear.

The presentation here is systematic, and thoughtful, but not academic or comprehensive. I have not attempted a complete or planned study of spoken and written English. The corpus involved has been my usual diet of conversation, reading matter and television; from staffroom

3

anecdote, literature (serious and lurid), and dramatic performance (from classic theatre to soap opera). Nor have I recorded every odd expression I have heard - most yes, but when a pen was not to hand memory did not always suffice. Friends tend to become suspicious, not to say hostile, if you start writing down things they have just said!

Finally, I am not an academic 'grammarian'. I have taught EFL and written EFL materials. My main preoccupation, therefore, is with the influence on language teaching of various grammatical descriptions and approaches, rather than the search for grammatical truth for its own sake. What I regard as important is that grammatical explanations used in language teaching should in fact provide an accurate reflection of what native speakers say rather than some simplified half-truth that has been devised because it is 'easier'.

I also feel that it is important that language teachers and grammarians continue to pay attention to developments in the use of English and the language change that is continually taking place around them. Teachers should be prepared to adjust and adapt their teaching to take their own observations into account. Grammarians can, and should, give them the necessary theoretical support, but nothing can help teachers who do not observe with interest the language around them.

The three things we all need are: open ears, open eyes and, most important of all, an open mind.

If you are reading a detective story or a thriller, you will probably not welcome anyone who divulges the ending before you get there yourself. However, there are other situations - and reading this book is one of them - when it may be useful to know what the ending will be, or at least what points will be made along the way. The arguments put forward will therefore, I hope, be easier to follow and the direction I am heading in that much clearer. There are five main points I wish to make:

Language Awareness

More importance must be attached to language awareness. The underlying theme of the whole book is to emphasise how important language awareness is. It affects our

'Open ears, open eyes, and an open mind'.

perceptions of language and the way we describe it, and it influences language teaching and how teachers deal with language in the classroom.

Observation of 'real' language

Observation of 'real' language is essential. For too long language teachers have relied on 'received' descriptions of the language rather than accounts of what speakers and writers of English actually produce. In many cases reference books are researched by referring to other reference books, rather than by referring to the language itself. In this way unreliable explanations get handed down for some considerable time. Other works draw their conclusions directly from a corpus of material and obviously claim greater authority on account of this. But even they will be limited by the finite nature of their corpus, however large it may be. While the books that so many of us constantly consult are useful aids, they should not be seen as representing or conveying ultimate grammatical truth. They are fallible.

Language changes

Language changes. This is something that everyone agrees with in theory. However, when it comes to acknowledging a change in **current** usage many people show a marked reluctance. A popular stance seems to be that language changed in the past and that was quite acceptable, but what we say or write now is 'correct' and does not change. Later in the book we will look at a few areas where language can be seen to be changing.

A 'spectrum of likelihood'

The idea of language being 'right' or 'wrong' is not always very useful. Too often we become obsessed with whether a piece of language is 'correct' or 'incorrect'. As teachers we feel it necessary to provide absolute judgements when asked to do so. In reality there is a hard core of acceptability surrounded by a vast grey area. That grey area, however, cannot really be seen as 'unacceptable'. Native speakers will often argue over the acceptability of various items; grammarians themselves will be undecided; native speakers will often encroach into the grey area to express new, previously unexpressed, ideas. The grey area does not contain 'unacceptable' language, rather 'unlikely' language.

Michael Lewis has suggested the idea of a 'spectrum of likelihood'. At one end of the spectrum is the area of 'highly likely' (acceptable) language; at the other end is an area of 'very unlikely' (unacceptable) language; and in the middle is a wide range of possibilities of varying likelihood (varying acceptability). In short, 'likely' or 'unlikely' – which represent a **continuum** – are more useful concepts than the simple 'right' or 'wrong' opposition.

Teachers' own resources

Greater awareness of language has important implications for language teachers. At first it may seem frightening that we can no longer rely on our well-thumbed reference works to provide all the right answers. However, we may come to realise that we can rely more and more on our own resources and intuition and less and less on grammars and dictionaries. We will have to decide to what extent we can share our uncertainties with our students. And we will have to think carefully about how far our observations will influence our selection of the language that is to be taught.

PART ONE

BACKGROUND

CHAPTER ONE

LANGUAGE AWARENESS

It seems strange that a book intended for language teachers should start by stressing the need for language awareness. However, many teachers I know, myself included, get locked into the class we are teaching, the coursebook we are using, the structures we are introducing, to the extent that we do not give as much attention as we perhaps should to the normal language activity that takes place around us outside the classroom. This is odd because it is that very language activity that is providing the basis for what we teach inside the classroom.

Consider the following questions:

1.1 **A student has asked you to explain a difficult point of grammar, which you are not absolutely sure about. Do you**

- **a.** use your intuition to give the best answer you can and consult a reference book later to confirm your explanation?
- **b.** use your intuition to give the best answer you can and consult a colleague later to confirm your explanation?
- **c.** consult a reference book before giving an explanation?
- **d.** consult a colleague before giving an explanation?

1.2 **How often do you observe odd or interesting uses of language (either English or your mother tongue) outside the classroom**

- **a.** quite a few times every day?
- **b.** about once a day?
- **c.** occasionally?
- **d.** hardly ever?

There is, of course, no right answer to these questions, but one might draw some tentative conclusions from whatever you have chosen. If you have answered (c) or (d) to the first question, you should perhaps place more confidence in your intuition. Often, arriving at an explanation of a language problem involves nothing more than conducting a brief survey of one's own language experience. For a difficult point it is obviously wise to check with a reference work since that will, one hopes, be based on a broader range of language experience than any one person can hope to possess. However, that should not deny your own language experience; if a situation arises in which the reference work and your own intuition and experience are at odds with one another, it is my feeling that you should disregard the reference work. You may not agree at the moment - I hope you will by the end of this book.

If you have answered (a) or (b) to the first question you obviously have more confidence in your own intuition. Whether you decide to consult a reference work or a colleague probably makes little difference. However, consulting colleagues may provide a perspective that is not apparent in the reference work.

'Colleagues may provide a perspective that is not apparent in the reference work.'

It may, for example, indicate that where the reference work gives, say, a clear ruling on acceptability, there is in fact a large area of disagreement. That disagreement is something that we should be aware of. It is also something we should **not** be **afraid** of.

The second question is designed to make you aware of how perceptive you are about the language used around you. A good answer would be (a). To be honest, it is not something that I achieve. In my experience there are times when odd and unusual language crops up with alarming regularity - there may be five examples in one day, or ten in a week - and then there are barren periods when nothing unusual seems to happen for a long time. This probably has more to do with my own lack of alertness than the actual rate of occurrence. I suspect that careful and consistent study would reveal frequent unusual uses of language. Chapter 20, on data collection, certainly gives this impression. If you have answered (c) or (d), this suggests that you should pay more attention to the language around you. In Britain, for example, television news programmes are a frequent source of data; the newspapers too (many of which are available abroad) are often also a fund of interesting and unusual language use. If you are a (c) or a (d) type person, perhaps you should sit down for five or ten minutes with an English newspaper or in front of an English radio or television programme and consciously try to find an item of language that startles or surprises you. Disconcerting examples may be much more frequent than you expect!

CHAPTER TWO

GRAMMARS

Before going on to study the examples that I have collected, we should first look at the concept of grammar and the different attitudes that people take towards it. There are various different types of grammar, all of which have their uses and their drawbacks. Here we look at three different types which we will call **prescriptive, descriptive,** and **pedagogic**.

2.1 Prescriptive grammar

Prescriptive grammar, the sort which sets out to specify absolutely what is right and wrong, what one should or should not say, has these days largely been discredited from the point of view of language teaching. Books such as *The King's English* by H.W.Fowler and F.G.Fowler and *Usage and Abusage* by Eric Partridge are generally thought to be antiquarian in outlook and contain only a picture of what used to be considered correct English in the days when they were first written, 1906 and 1947 respectively. The latter contains such entries as:

> **patronize** for *trade with* (a grocer) or *at* (his shop) is commercial pretentiousness.

contact (v.) If you feel that without this American synonym for 'to establish contact with' or, more idiomatically, 'get in(to) touch with' [a person], life would be too unutterably dreary and bleak and 'grim', do at least say or write 'to contact a person', not *contact with*, as in John G. Brandon's "I've questioned every C.I.D. man I've contacted with."

Despite the unfashionability of prescriptive grammar, books like these contain much useful information about the history of the language and even about distinctions and meanings that are still in current use. However, they still set out to tell us what we should and should not say and in doing so fail to give a clear picture of what native speakers actually do say. They have also influenced generations into believing that there is a 'right' and 'wrong' way of writing or saying something, and that it is one of the functions of a grammar book to protect the language from incorrect use. This attitude is hopelessly reactionary.

2.2 Descriptive grammar

Descriptive grammar, describing the language rather than prescribing it, is what most language teachers and most contemporary grammarians are interested in. Books such as *A Comprehensive Grammar of the English Language* by Quirk, Greenbaum, Leech and Svartvik and its forerunner *A Grammar of Contemporary English* by the same authors offer a massive and well-researched description of English that has for many years rightly been considered the standard reference work for language teachers and grammarians alike.

There are, however, problems even with descriptive grammars. The first major snag is the notion of acceptability. Quirk et al. use elicitation experiments with native speakers in determining whether a form is acceptable and also point to a correlation between frequency and acceptability. The experiments are set up with the aim of eliciting particular forms from native speakers, thus confirming their acceptability. The correlation with frequency asserts that the more frequently a form appears, the more acceptable it is. The connection with frequency is important here and is something we shall return to later in the book. Exactly how frequent does a form have to be before it is considered acceptable? Quirk and associates do not say. If a form is infrequent, is it unacceptable? Or is it just unlikely?

The other big problem with descriptive grammars is the attitude of the reader. The grammar may indeed be descriptive. Readers may believe that their own attitude towards grammar is descriptive. Yet when they consult a grammar they will often regard their findings as the absolute unchangeable truth. In reality, however, language change may have outstripped the publisher's ability to keep up with it, or the point in question may not have been included in the grammar for a variety of reasons. Readers would do better to trust the evidence of their own eyes or ears as to what native speakers actually write or say. The grammar we use may indeed be descriptive. We should make sure our attitude towards it is too, and that we are not falling into the prescriptivist role that most of us claim to be keen to avoid.

2.3 Pedagogic grammar

Pedagogic grammar is generally distinguished by the fact that the explanations, and probably the scope, have been simplified or put into a more digestible form for the benefit of the learner. In some ways this is a laudable principle. It makes no sense to explain *some* and *any*, say, in terms which the learner does not understand. But is it good practice to tell learners that we use *some* in positive sentences and *any* in negatives and questions when this is patently not true? It may seem to be a useful, pedagogically justified simplification, but in the long run the learner's task will be made more difficult. It will undoubtedly lead to students producing odd utterances and acquiring a habit that they will later have to get rid of.

As a teacher it goes against the grain professionally to

suggest that another teacher has not told students the correct rules. Unfortunately, that becomes necessary if students are to come to terms with examples that fall outside the scope of incomplete rules they have previously been taught. Rather than concentrating on excessive simplification, pedagogic grammars should be concerned with what actually happens in language. That would make both the learner's and the teacher's task easier.

This notion may, at first acquaintance, appear eccentric, but it has a sound foundation in the theory of English Language Teaching. R.A.Close (1962) says of the rules for *some* and *any* given above:

> 'Hours are wasted not only on lessons teaching half-truths as if they were the whole truth, but also doing exercises which require the student to choose between two constructions, both of which can be perfectly acceptable, though one of the two is falsely supposed to be 'wrong'... Expressions like *'Would you like some more tea?'* and *'Any child could tell you that.'* both perfectly good English, would therefore be considered incorrect.'

He goes on to say 'Above all, an inadequate basic rule will sooner or later have to be modified by a series of sub-rules and exceptions which may cause far more trouble in the end than a basic rule that is more accurate though less temptingly teachable'.

This may go some way towards explaining why, having first been told that light travelled in straight lines and then later that it travelled in waves, I finally gave up on the laws of physics!

If we want to help students as much as possible, we should not undermine their confidence with half-truths subject to innumerable exceptions and alterations. As far as possible, we should provide a complete and accurate description of what really happens, as a sound foundation on which they can build.

CHAPTER THREE

INFLUENCES

While we are observing language, there are many factors that we must take into account. Some will affect our view of the acceptability of an utterance; some will exert such influence that the language can actually be deemed to have changed; some will be transitory and disappear as quickly as they arrived. I look at three of these factors below.

3.1 Slang

Slang is defined in many ways but for present purposes can be considered as highly colloquial language that is usually considered 'uneducated' or 'bad'. As a result of the accelerated speed of communications in the twentieth century, slang comes and goes at an even faster rate than it used to. From time to time slang words make their way up the ladder to acceptability. The noun 'mob' started out as a slang word but is now in perfectly acceptable usage. A number of expressions from Cockney rhyming slang have already become acceptable colloquialisms - rather than slang. 'To scarper' (Scapa Flow - go), 'use your loaf' (loaf of bread - head) have a small degree of respectability. Perhaps in time they will become fully acceptable.

The vast majority of slang, however, is transitory. Its influence is largely short term. In addition, it may be restricted to a certain class or group of people - young people in particular are prolific users and inventors of slang. As observers of language we must not be too hasty in identifying something as a change when it may in fact be a temporary slang usage. There are, for example, a number of words over the past twenty years or so which have all been used to mean 'good' - 'fab', 'real', 'groovy', 'far out', 'brilliant' and even 'bad' and 'wicked'! All of them have fallen into disuse, with the exceptions of 'brilliant' and 'bad'. These two are still current but the likelihood must be that they, too, will be replaced within a few years.

It is a long climb up the ladder from slang, to colloquialism, to acceptable usage, and we must make sure we do not fall into the trap of thinking that a transitory slang usage is a lasting language change. How we reach this decision is something I will return to when discussing acceptability.

3.2 Current obsessions

Another difficult area arises when a particular language change becomes either clichéd, or classified as 'uneducated' by those that regard themselves as 'educated'. Words such as 'hopefully' and 'situation', to name only a couple, often arouse major disapproval from listeners or readers if they are not used in their 'correct' sense.

'Hopefully', some people maintain, should not be used in the sense of 'it is hoped' but should qualify a verb. 'He smiled hopefully ...' is thought correct; 'The new legislation, hopefully, will lead to some improvements ...' is not.

To talk of a 'crisis situation' when we mean a crisis, and a 'holiday situation' when we mean on holiday is also thought wrong. However, neither of these examples can, in purely grammatical terms, be considered unacceptable. There are many other adverbs which stand on their own without qualifying a verb - for example, 'obviously' and 'ideally', so why not 'hopefully'? One can talk about 'the economic situation', why not 'a crisis situation'?

Splitting infinitives and putting prepositions at the end of sentences are also often frowned upon, despite the fact that there are sometimes good reasons for doing these things. Even Partridge (1975), who very much likes to lay down the law, writes: 'Avoid the split infinitive wherever possible: but if it is the clearest and the most natural construction, use it boldly' and '... too great a fear of putting the preposition at the end sometimes leads to even worse errors.' He goes on to quote H.W. Fowler as writing 'Those who lay down the universal principle that final prepositions are "inelegant" are unconsciously trying to deprive the English language of a valuable idiomatic resource.'

As students of language change, we must not be put off by the prescriptivist attitudes put forward in such cases. In many cases the real objection is not one of acceptability but of style. Those who object to a particular usage are frequently expressing no more than a personal prejudice - something like 'I don't say that, so other people shouldn't use the language like that either'!

While the language observed may not be the language that we would have chosen to use, it is necessary to remain detached and observe it as it is. As teachers we may try to discourage it; as observers we should note it. It may be an entirely new usage, in which case we will have to see if it occurs again. It may be a usage that is becoming more likely rather than less likely, in which case we will have to consider what effect that may have on our teaching.

3.3 American influences

Another area of influence on language change is American usage. The vast import of American print, video and audio material ensures considerable exposure to American English throughout not only Britain but the whole English speaking (and much of the non-English speaking) world. Phrases like 'to meet with' as opposed to 'to meet'; to 'talk with' rather than 'to talk to' are becoming common in British usage. The American use of the simple past where British English uses the present perfect is beginning to creep into British usage. It even seems to have found its way into a British coursebook (Anita Pacione's *Break into English Practice Book 2*, Hodder & Stoughton 1986):

I already <u>told</u> Jane about the party.

However, judging from an article by Simon Hoggart in The Observer magazine (1990), the linguistic traffic is not all one way. Many British expressions are now becoming commonplace in the United States. It seems that Americans now talk about the 'fridge' rather than the 'icebox'. They say 'pricey' instead of 'expensive'. Expressions such as 'smarmy', 'trendy' and 'early on' are gaining in popularity. This just adds to the confusion.

It is also worth pointing out that many American words and expressions are in fact derived from 16th and 17th century English. The use of 'guess' meaning 'suppose' goes back to the 14th century. Other archaic forms include 'mad' in the sense of 'angry', 'gotten' instead of 'got', and 'fall' instead of 'autumn'. For people who believe that 'underground' is British English and 'subway' American, it may come as a surprise to discover that the Victorian underground system of Glasgow has always been known as the 'subway'. Other grammatical differences thought to be peculiarly American, are standard in Scottish English and many English dialects. For example, the past participle form of 'prove' in Scotland is 'proven' (see Chapter 6 on the simple past).

All this adds up to a situation of some complexity which needs careful handling when it comes to observation of the language and discussion of possible change. This variety of language use, however, makes it a rich and fascinating area of study.

PART TWO

DATA

In this part of the book we will look more closely at some of the data I have collected. In some places - comparatives, for example - there are strong indications that the language is changing and that the standard grammatical explanations no longer apply. In other areas - adverbs, in particular - common preconceptions do not appear to be borne out by the evidence. Elsewhere - prepositions especially - it is likely that the rules we often find in reference works are not as fixed as they might seem. And looking further, there are places where all but the most comprehensive grammars fail to account for particular grammatical structures - word order is a good example of this.

All the data presented in this part of the book is authentic.* The references are quoted - usually at the end of each section. Each section will ask you to perform one or two tasks. Try to work through the tasks in order.

Editor's Note: The author wrote *All the data . . . is.* An example of the language change he discusses!

CHAPTER FOUR

COMPARATIVES

4.1 What is wrong with the following sentences?

a. 'Britain's political class seems more keen to be entertained than informed ...'

b. 'You ... must make the ascent ... along ninety miles of roads that grow more and more steep.'

c. 'Jeff gets more posh all the time.'

d. 'Just to make this wonderfully more clear of course, they've changed the system.'

e. 'We've been more full I must say, much more full in the last three weeks.'

f. 'It is definitely cheaper and more fresh.'

g. 'What I consider to be more grave is the theft of child benefit.'

h. 'It's not like a job on the Stock Exchange, but it's more sure.'

i. 'It was more clear than usual.'

4.2 Look at the references below which indicate where these sentences came from. Are your answers to question one still the same?

a. The Spectator (a weekly magazine). 1.3.1986. from an article by Peregrine Worsthorne.

b. Great Railway Journeys of the World. Brian Thompson. Sphere 1982.

c. Ripley Under Ground. Patricia Highsmith. Heinemann 1971.

d. Progress Towards First Certificate. Leo Jones. CUP 1983.

e. Conversation on a train. 30.11.1987.

f. Living Decisions: People At Home. (Educational TV programme) BBC2. 2.3.1988.

g. Neil Kinnock. House Of Commons. 27.10.1988.

h. The Independent. 13.2.1989.

i. ITN News, 27.10.1989.

4.3 Which of the following grammar explanations account completely for the sentences above?

> (Adjectives of one syllable) form comparatives and superlatives with *-er, -est*.

Practical English Usage. Swan. OUP. 1980.

> The following kinds of adjective form the comparative and superlative by adding *-er* and *-est*: monosyllables

Cassell's Students' English Grammar. Allsop. Cassell. 1983.

> One syllable words normally take the inflected forms.
> Exceptions to the inflection rule . . . are
> (a) past participles
> (b) ungradable adjectives . . .

Current English Grammar. Chalker. Macmillan. 1984.

> Most adjectives that are inflected for comparison can also take the periphrastic forms with *more* and *most*. With *more* they seem to do so more easily when they are predicative and are followed by a than clause.

A Comprehensive Grammar of the English Language. Quirk, Greenbaum, Leech & Svartvik. Longman 1985.

4.4 Consider the following:

a. How often must we come across this structure for it to be regarded as acceptable?

b. Should we continue to tell students that the sentences in question one are unacceptable?

c. Is it acceptable to teach students rules which are contradicted by current use?

d. Should we teach the structure illustrated as passive knowledge, and if so to what level of student?

e. Should we teach the structure illustrated as active knowledge, and if so to what level of student?

f. Should we correct the structure when students produce it?

g. Should we penalise students who produce the structure in a test or exam?

h. Will students be penalised if they produce the structure in an external examination?

4.5 In the light of the information above, what rules for the formation of comparatives should be taught to foreign learners at:

a. elementary level?

....

....

....

b. intermediate level?

....

....

....

c. advanced level?

....

....

....

My feeling is that this area is one where it is not too difficult for people to accept change. The difference between 'clearer' and 'more clear' is not that great. The use of 'more' to make comparatives is well established with longer adjectives, and frequent with two-syllable adjectives. It is in some measure a logical progression. One possible reason for the change is the tendency in English for inflections to disappear. The present simple, for example, has gradually been losing inflections and with full verbs has only the 3rd person 's' left. The disappearance of '-er' and '-est' can reasonably be seen as part of a similar process. On the other hand, another possibility is that the use of 'more' with monosyllables gives greater emphasis to the comparative.

However reasonable it is, though, the problems that it raises are outlined in question four. These are questions that are thrown up by all the data in this book and we will return to them in Part Three when we consider the implications of language change in greater depth.

Meanwhile, in the light of the examples above, how would you react to this authentic test item?

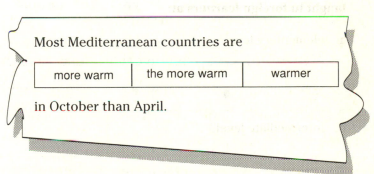

Most Mediterranean countries are		
more warm	the more warm	warmer

in October than April.

Dave Allan. Oxford Placement Test 2. OUP 1985.

CHAPTER FIVE

PREPOSITIONS

Some time ago a student in one of my classes asked which preposition followed the adjective *'helpful'*. *'For'* I replied, as the sentence *'This book will be helpful for my exams'* popped into my head. *'But it says 'to' in my dictionary,'* continued the student. And sure enough it did! *'Well 'to' is possible'*, I bluffed (keeping my fingers crossed). I made a mental note to check in the break. When I did so, no dictionary allowed *'for'* as a preposition with *'helpful'*, but the staff were in unanimous agreement - a most unusual event - that it was acceptable.

5.1 **Which prepositions would you use? Choose one (a, b, c or d) to complete each sentence.**

1. The Bradford City chairman has admitted that, ... hindsight, there were other things that could have been done.
    (a) in   **(b)** with   **(c)** by   **(d)** from

2. This model makes much greater demands ..... individual teachers.
    (a) on   **(b)** of   **(c)** with   **(d)** to

3. I should like to congratulate the BBC ..... this programme.
    (a) on   **(b)** to   **(c)** for   **(d)** with

4. It's one problem there's no solution ..... .
    (a) with   **(b)** by   **(c)** to   **(d)** for

5. Your room and the suite together were more or less identical ..... the sitting room, then?
    (a) by   **(b)** to   **(c)** with   **(d)** of

6. Suitable ..... plates but not ovenware.
   (a) of   **(b)** from   **(c)** for   **(d)** to

7. How do you get to Telford ..... emergencies?
   (a) of   **(b)** under   **(c)** in   **(d)** with

8. Do you surround yourself ..... bodyguards?
   (a) by   **(b)** with   **(c)** for   **(d)** of

9. It could save Lord Mackay ..... having to resign.
   (a) -   **(b)** from   **(c)** of   **(d)** by

10. It was quite interesting ..... me to see Wilcox in his
    domestic setting.
    (a) to   **(b)** in   **(c)** with   **(d)** for

5.2 **Check your answers with the key below.**

These prepositions are those that were actually used:

1. in	**5.** with	**8.** by
2. of	**6.** to	**9.** of
3. for	**7.** under	**10.** to
4. for		

How many did you get right?

5.3 **Now check the answers above and your own answers with the recommendations of a variety of dictionaries on the next page.**

Another source of information is, of course, colleagues. With a language that is constantly changing and with reference books that do not always supply completely satisfactory answers, colleagues provide an up-to-date and invaluable yardstick. I conducted a spot survey on the first

DICTIONARY TABLE

	OALDCE	LDOCE	OSDCE	COBUILD	SOED	KEY
1.	with	–	–	–	–	in
2.	of/on	on	on	of	–	of
3.	on	on	on	on/for	on	for
4.	to	–	to	of/for	for	for
5.	to/with	with(to?)	–	to/with	–	with
6.	for/to	for	for	for	to/for	to
7.	in	in	in	in	–	under
8.	with	–	with(by?)	with(by?)	–	by
9.	from	from	from	from	from	of
10.	–	–	–	–	to	to

OALDCE – Oxford Advanced Learner's Dictionary of Current English (4th Edition)
LDOCE – Longman Dictionary of Contemporary English
OSDCE – Oxford Student's Dictionary of Current English (2nd Edition)
SOED – Shorter Oxford English Dictionary (3rd Edition)
COBUILD – Collins Cobuild English Language Dictionary

four sentences above, asking teachers to imagine the sentences had been produced by a student and to decide on their acceptability. **There was no unanimous agreement on even one of them!**

All except one person thought (2) was unacceptable; a good majority considered (1) unacceptable; opinion on (3) and (4) was divided roughly equally.

5.4 Consider the following questions:

a. How reliable are dictionaries when it comes to judging the acceptability of prepositions?

b. How reliable is your own intuition when it comes to judging the acceptability of prepositions?

c. What other sources of information can you think of for verifying the acceptability of prepositions?

d. What procedure would you recommend to students wanting to check a particular prepositional usage?

e. How do you feel about the teaching of prepositions in the light of the information presented here?

5.5 Try out your own research. Here are another six examples with their sources. How do you feel about them? What do your reference sources say?

11. We have been brought here today on false pretences.

12. Rangers players are rumoured to have been forbidden from seeing *My Left Foot*.

13. Can we take it the Iran government is serious on this?

14. I telephoned to his accountant.

15. She was a mainliner because dragon chasing and mouth organ playing were no longer sufficient to her.

16. Have you an explanation of this?

Most of the above information was presented as a poster at the IATEFL conference in Dublin in April 1990. There was also a blank sheet attached to the poster for people to write their comments on. One or two people were rather upset by the sentences; some contesting that they were 'wrong' rather than very unusual or unlikely. But not everyone. The most interesting comments came from Seth Lindstromberg and are reproduced opposite.

References
1. BBC 1 News - 6.12.1985
2. A speaker at the IATEFL conference - 11.4.1988
3. Letter to 'Points of View' - 27.4.1988
4. Coronation Street (ITV) - 11.5.1988
5. Hot Money. Dick Francis. Pan Books. 1988
6. Notice in Department Store. 26.10.1988
7. BBC Radio 4 - 10.5.1989
8. Michael Aspel. ITV. 7.10.1988
9. BBC Radio 4 - 24.5.1989
10. David Lodge. Nice Work. Penguin 1989.
11. BBC1 News 17.11.1989.
12. The Independent 31.3.1990.
13. BBC Six O'Clock News. 11.4.1990.
14. Dick Francis. Straight. Michael Joseph. 1989
15. Gerald Seymour. Home Run. Fontana 1989.
16. Pocketful of Rye. Agatha Christie. BBC1 14.7.1990.

Prepositions are <u>not</u> "delexicalized forms". They are <u>not</u> well described when they are called "function" words. Each preposition has its own meaning i.e. conveys a different image. If people use one rather than another, it's because they are conceiving of the relationship in question in a particular way. Often, more than one way is possible for any (gapped) context... decisions about which preposition to use are only <u>partly</u> determined by collocational habits ... not crucially so determined either.

e.g.

   "in an emergency" – metaphor of an emergency as a trap?

"under an emergency" – an emergency as something pressing down, a weight, an incubus

None of the choices, either those of the dictionaries or of the sources are exceptional seen in this light. In my opinion anyway.

What do you think?

CHAPTER SIX

THE SIMPLE PAST

If we agree that acceptability and frequency are related and that the more frequently an item occurs the more acceptable it is, we are often doing no more than the average language teacher when they are asked if something is correct or not. We draw on our own experience, think of all the language we have come across, and pronounce an utterance acceptable or unacceptable, likely or unlikely. Frequency as a key idea is useful. Native-speaker intuition as a gauge of frequency is also useful, but not necessarily infallible.

6.1 **Are these sentences right or wrong?**

1. Inside the glass enclosure Joel lighted a cigarette, thinking about what he was going to say.

2. Drivers weaved their way around fallen trees.

3. I've just waked up to the kind of imbecile nonsense that my life has become.

In fact research in a range of dictionaries shows that all these sentences are correct. *Lighted* is a possible, but unusual, simple past form of *light*. *Weaved* is the correct past tense form of *weave* when it means 'to move by twisting' (Oxford Advanced Learner's Dictionary). *Waked* is a possible past tense form of *wake* (archaic according to the Oxford Advanced Learner's Dictionary, but American usage according to COBUILD.)

6.2 **Now test your own past tense and past participle forms and see how many you can complete in the table below.**

INFINITIVE	SIMPLE PAST	PAST PARTICIPLE
light	lit lighted	lit lighted
weave		
wake		
lean		
shine		
swell		
speed		
dive		
prove		
blow		
hang		
beseech		
spell		
bet		
quit		

6.3 Now check your answers in the table below.

INFINITIVE	SIMPLE PAST	PAST PARTICIPLE
light	lit lighted	lit lighted
weave	wove weaved[1]	woven weaved[1]
wake	woke waked[2]	waken waked[2]
lean	leaned leant	leaned leant
shine	shone shined[1]	shone shined[1]
swell	swelled	swelled swollen
speed	sped speeded[1]	sped speeded[1]
dive	dived dove[3]	dived
prove	proved	proved proven[3]
blow	blew	blown blowed[4]
hang	hung hanged[1]	hung hanged[1]
beseech	beseeched besought	beseeched besought
spell	spelled spelt	spelled spelt
bet	bet betted	bet betted[5]
quit	quit quitted	quit quitted[5]

1. These are only possible with certain meanings of the word.
2. This usage is either archaic or American depending which dictionary you consult. See above.
3. American usage.
4. *'Blowed'* exists but only in the idiomatic *'Well, I'll be blowed'* and similar expressions.
5. COBUILD gives only *bet* and *quit.*

Apart from the notes above, all the variations are equally possible. If you got them all, you will have done very well. Variations like *spelled* and *spelt* are reasonably common, but others are less so. The Oxford Advanced Learner's Dictionary lists over fifty verbs that have possible variations in either the simple past, the past participle or both. I chose some of the more common ones above. But you can do your own research. *Cleave,* for example, has four possible simple past forms and three possible past participle forms. How many can you think of?

The point of this exercise is really a warning. I recorded the three examples at the beginning of this chapter because I thought they were deviant. In fact when I came to look at them more closely and check the authorities, I found out that they were not that unusual at all. It was my own inexperience or ignorance! If you come across a piece of language that seems strange, you should first check. It might well be quite acceptable, even quite likely, but merely outside the realm of your experience.

References
1. The Aquitaine Progression, Robert Ludlum. Panther Books 1985
2. BBC1, Nine O'Clock News, 16/10/87
3. Joyce Cary, The Breakout from The Penguin Book of English Short Stories, Penguin 1967

CHAPTER SEVEN

ADVERBS

> # PLEASE DRIVE SLOW
> # CHILDREN PLAYING

One area of language that many people think is suffering abuse, especially in American English, is adverbs. A number of people have suggested to me that Americans often seem to use the adjectival form rather than the adverbial form that British English prefers. The impression these people give is that the large number of television programmes shown here in Britain seems to be influencing British English. In addition, this use of the adjectival form is seen as a negative development. It is a practice which people seem to associate with 'lack of education'. Adverbs, therefore, constituted one area that I was particularly conscious of when keeping an ear or an eye open for interesting material. What I discovered was actually quite surprising. Look at the question below:

How do you feel about these British-English sentences?

1. The most powerful way of getting the message through clearer.

2. How do you feel when a foreigner pronounces your name wrong.

3. Please drive slow. Children playing.

4. Jack could hear him snoring very loud.

5. Its authors ... have produced a document three times as long... and much worse written.

6. I want a completion as quick as possible.

I consulted Swan (1980), COBUILD (1990) and Quirk et al. (1985). All the sentences above are correct. The first sentence is probably the most difficult to account for, but Quirk et al. say:

> Whereas *clear* is non-standard for *clearly,* [clearer] and [clearest] are both acceptable standard English variants of *more clearly* and *most clearly,* respectively.

'*Wrong', 'slow', 'loud'* and '*quick'* are all listed by Swan and COBUILD as adverbs which have the same form as their adjectives. There are actually more of these than you might think. Swan lists 34 and COBUILD 47.

The fifth example sounds awful in my opinion but none of the reference works suggest it is unacceptable. My objection must be stylistic then rather than grammatical.

There are a number of points that arise here. First the number of adverbs that can have the same form as their adjective. Quirk et al. write:

> In standard use, only a limited number of adverbs are formally identical to adjectives.

and later:

> ... in non-standard or very familiar English the use of the adjective for the adverb form is widespread.

Yet this is really just a matter of degree. To Quirk et al. it is a limited number; I would call it a large number. The COBUILD list looks like this:

alike	fine	just	off-hand	solo
allright	first	kindly	only	still
alone	free	last	outright	straight
clean	freelance	late	overall	tight
deep	full	little	part-time	well
direct	full-time	long	past	wide
even	further	loud	pretty	wrong
extra	hard	low	quick	
far	high	next	right	
fast	jolly	non-stop	slow	

The result of this may well be that people who are concerned about grammatical usage are assuming wrongly that the correct use of the adverb is declining. It is more likely that they are unaware of the extent to which it is possible to use the adjectival form as an adverb. The instances above would certainly seem to suggest that. As in the previous chapter I stress that what may seem unlikely or unusual to some people is not necessarily unacceptable. The language experience of any individual is a minute fraction of what goes to make up contemporary English. It is curiously arrogant to translate *'I've never heard it before'* to *'It doesn't exist'* or, worse still, *'It's wrong'*.

References
1. A speaker at the IATEFL conference, Edinburgh 1988
2. Joanne Kenworthy. Teaching English Pronunciation. Longman 1987
3. Pub car park notice. Long Preston. 1.5.1988
4. Old MacDonald Had A Farm. ELC cassette.
5. The Independent. 27.4.1988
6. Coronation Street. ITV. 6.6.1990

CHAPTER EIGHT

CONDITIONAL SENTENCES

8.1 **How many types of conditional do you think there are? List as many types as you can before reading on.**

Conditionals are a notoriously tricky area for both teachers and students. They are also an area where considerable confusion is caused by the efforts of some teachers and grammarians to simplify matters in order to make them 'easier' for students. As a result, teachers can find themselves with a class of students some of whom think there are three conditionals (first, second and third), some of whom think there are four (first, second, third and zero!) and some of whom think there are two (real/open and unreal/hypothetical).

There is also often a profusion of 'rules' - you cannot have '*will*' in the *if*-clause; you cannot have '*would*' in the *if*-clause, etc.

With so much confusion as a starting point, it becomes difficult to monitor language which seems unusual. If we used the explanations in one or two well-known grammars as a yardstick of acceptability, we would fill a book this size with seemingly unacceptable language in a remarkably short time. By the same token it becomes difficult to spot language change - after all, do we mean change from what the grammars say, or change from what people actually say, and perhaps have been saying for some time?

8.2 **What is your attitude to these examples?**

There is, however, one area where change does seem to be taking place and because of the grammatical problems it throws up, it is quite controversial. Consider the following sentences:

1.

> # "If we'd have found
> an unsafe microwave oven,
> we would have named it.
> But we haven't found
> an unsafe microwave oven."
>
> Steve James, who carried out the Government tests on microwave ovens
> at The Institute of Food Research, talking on BBCTV

2. We wouldn't have met if he hadn't've done it.

3. If I'd've thought, we could've done something else.

4. If anything'd have happened to me, I would have been surrounded by protectors.

5. If he'd've been there, she'd've gone her own way more often.

6. If she had have told you she was giving up Sir Alan Walters, you would have stayed.

(see page 43 for sources)

One problem that immediately arises is that five of the six examples are spoken English - though all spoken by educated native speakers; the other, from the ITV drama *Wreath of Roses*, adapted from Elizabeth Taylor's novel, is also spoken English, but English that has been scripted to be spoken. Whilst it is easy to argue that native-speakers often make slips in conversation and that the offending *have* in the *if*-clauses above is just a slip, it is more difficult to do so with example 2. It is also interesting that the Daily Mail did not see fit to 'correct' the words of the spokesman it was quoting in the first example.

A look at various reference books proves interesting. Neither Chalker (1984) nor Allsop (1983) make any mention of this structure in conditionals. Quirk et al.(1985) refer to the extra *have* in a footnote and describe it as 'informal American English'. They also assert that *I'd've* in the *if*-clause is in fact *I would have* rather than *I had have,* which is 'an error that is found in uneducated writing'. This view may once have been true but seems now to fly in the face of the evidence of sentences 2 and 6. Michael Swan (1980) says 'This is considered "incorrect", and is not normally written, but *it is common even in educated people's speech.*' (my italics). And interestingly, Julie Spencer in a letter to Practical English Teaching (June 1987) notes '... it is surprising just how many examples you can find.' So despite the absence of any mention in Allsop and Chalker, it would seem that the presence of *have* after *had* in *if*-clauses does occur ... but how acceptable is it, and how, as teachers, should we deal with it?

Taking a broad view of the little information that there is in the reference works, it seems that this particular usage is informal, of American origin, almost entirely used in spoken English only, and now used reasonably widely amongst native-speakers. I agree with Julie Spencer about the surprising number of examples that crop up, but I was interested to notice that she referred only to spoken English. I too have not recorded a single written example - except perhaps those two listed above (numbers 1 and 2). On the subject of acceptability, Michael Swan, from his use of inverted commas around the word 'incorrect', obviously regards it as a valid part of native-speaker usage rather than incorrect. A view with which I agree - after all, what frequency of use is necessary for a structure to become acceptable?

Given, then, that this variation of the conditional has a degree of respectability, and occurs with some frequency in the 'educated' variety of spoken English that we generally teach our pupils, this poses questions similar to those we considered in the chapter on comparatives.

8.3 Consider the following questions:

a. Since the structure is reasonably frequent in 'educated' speech, are we justified in continuing to regard it as unacceptable?
b. Should we continue to tell students that the structure is unacceptable?
c. Should we teach the structure as passive knowledge, and if so, to what level of student?
d. Should we teach the structure as active knowledge, and if so, to what level of student?

e. Should we correct the structure when students produce it?

f. Should we penalise students if they produce the structure in an exam?

g. Should students be penalised if they produce the structure in an external oral exam?

As we said at the beginning of this chapter, conditionals are a notoriously tricky area. Attempts to simplify the 'rules' and make things 'easier' for the learner generally fail. This is largely because the combination of tenses and modals possible in the *if*-clause and the main clause is extremely large - much larger than can be accounted for by the traditional first, second, third conditional idea. Even adding the zero conditional does not help much.

8.4 **Have a look at the sentences below and see if your own theory of conditionals can account for all of them? If not, can you amend your theory so that it does?**

7. But you won't close the Dragons down either - even if you'll be able to prove it, which I doubt.

8. If you wouldn't splash, it wouldn't go in your eyes,' she just caught him say.

9. We'll split the swag, if you'll help.

10. If they'll shoot him, they'll shoot anyone.

11. If the Privy Council appeals succeed, he would probably be a free man.

12. ... but I couldn't bear to go to his house and see Moira smirking in Coochie's place, even if he would have let me in through the door.

13. If heaven lay about her in her infancy, Victoria Wood can be excused for not noticing.

14. If it would be fun to do it, I would do it.

15. I'll be very surprised if I won this.

It would be wonderfully convenient if we could assert that all conditional sentences which did not conform to, say, the first-second-third type rules were unacceptable. It would vastly simplify the teaching and learning of conditionals. It would also provide students with an absurdly unrepresentative picture of what 'real' English, written and spoken, is like.

Penny Ur in a letter to ELT Journal (ELT Journal 43/1) reported the results of a mini-survey carried out on the patterns of frequency of different conditional forms in written English. She writes:

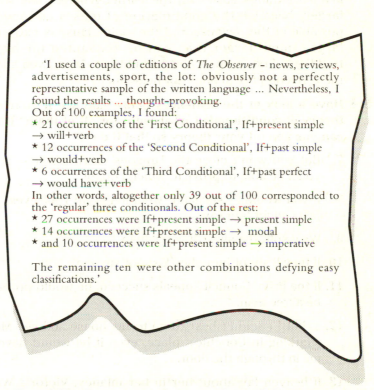

'I used a couple of editions of *The Observer* – news, reviews, advertisements, sport, the lot: obviously not a perfectly representative sample of the written language ... Nevertheless, I found the results ... thought-provoking.
Out of 100 examples, I found:
* 21 occurrences of the 'First Conditional', If+present simple → will+verb
* 12 occurrences of the 'Second Conditional', If+past simple → would+verb
* 6 occurrences of the 'Third Conditional', If+past perfect → would have+verb
In other words, altogether only 39 out of 100 corresponded to the 'regular' three conditionals. Out of the rest:
* 27 occurrences were If+present simple → present simple
* 14 occurrences were If+present simple → modal
* and 10 occurrences were If+present simple → imperative

The remaining ten were other combinations defying easy classifications.'

David Maule in an earlier article in ELT Journal (ELT Journal 42/2) conducted a similar survey of spoken English in which 'Of the 100 sentences gathered, a staggering total of 7 conformed to the standard Type 1 If + Present Simple→ will + verb pattern so beloved of coursebooks and pedagogic grammars. What was rather more significant was that 14 - exactly twice that number - were of the If + Present Simple→ Present Simple pattern' and 'Aside from these two

groups there were another 40 real non-past conditionals which made use of present tenses, the imperative, modals, be to, have to, have got to, going to, etc.'

In the face of this sort of evidence, and assuming that throwing up our hands in despair is not an option, what should we as teachers do about the teaching of conditionals? Penny Ur continues her letter by arguing the merits of continuing to teach the three conditionals. 'These are, for most students, far more difficult to internalize and use than the various 'non-conventional' forms, and do occur often enough to be considered an essential component of the English language.'

Though she continues 'we should at the same time make our students aware that many other types of *If* clauses are possible, acceptable, and frequent.' David Maule concludes 'Too much emphasis on the idea that there is a standard structure for each 'type' places unnecessary restraint on the students' natural curiosity and communicative ability. This may even lead to the rejection of perfectly valid alternative forms.'

Swan (1980) and Chalker (1984) prefer to divide conditionals into two types 'real' and 'unreal' (Swan), and 'open' and 'hypothetical' (Chalker). And Swan and Walter in The Cambridge English Course use this division for teaching purposes.

My feeling is that the division into two is more pedagogically useful than the division into three in that it encompasses more of what Penny Ur describes as 'non-conventional' forms. This leaves fewer forms unaccounted for. Ultimately, however, each individual will take a variety of factors into consideration when deciding how to present conditionals - the students, their first language, their current language level, what he or she feels happy with as a grammatical explanation, the materials to be used, etc. What the teacher cannot do though is present the first, second and third conditionals as the only possible forms in English.

References
1. Daily Mail (verbatim report) 9.12.1989
2. Elizabeth Taylor. Wreath of Roses. TV adaptation of her novel. 1987
3. Informal conversation 10.10.1987
4. BBC1. Wogan 8.4.1988
5. Informal conversation 6.10.1985
6. Brian Walden. The Walden Interview. ITV 5.11.1989
7. James Clavell. Noble House. Hodder & Stoughton 1981
8. Graham Swift. Learning To Swim. Pan Books. 1985
9. Caption from 'The Tramp' starring Charlie Chaplin. 1915
10. James Clavell. Whirlwind. Coronet. 1986
11. Letter to The Independent. 7.3.1988
12. Dick Francis. Hot Money. Pan Books 1988.
13. The Times 28.10.89
14. BBC1. Wogan. 5.1.90
15. The Independent. 8.9.1990

CHAPTER NINE

THE APOSTROPHE

Given that frequency is a criterion for acceptability, one of the most frequent occurences that I have observed is the 'misuse' of the apostrophe. It occurs more frequently than any other of the observations in this book. As a change of use, if indeed it is, it arouses strong opinions in almost everyone - and on occasions stimulates correspondence in the national press. Where do you stand?

9.1 **Read the dialogue below.**

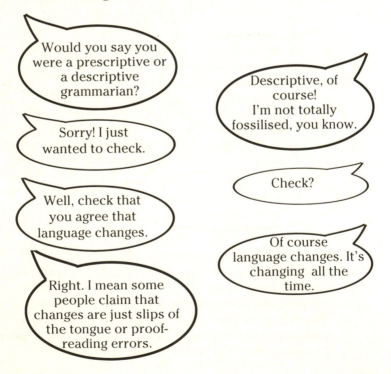

Would you say you were a prescriptive or a descriptive grammarian?

Descriptive, of course! I'm not totally fossilised, you know.

Sorry! I just wanted to check.

Check?

Well, check that you agree that language changes.

Of course language changes. It's changing all the time.

Right. I mean some people claim that changes are just slips of the tongue or proof-reading errors.

Well, yes - they do occur. But once there are frequent examples of a change, we must recognise it as such.

Oh! I agree entirely. And ... with both spoken and written language.

And punctuation ...

Certainly. With spoken language the changes seem to happen faster; but they do happen in written language too.

Sure. I mean, look at formal letters. You used to have to indent every paragraph. And now you don't.

A good example. Of course, most people take a descriptive view of grammar now, don't they?

Oh! I think almost everyone. Certainly all the major grammar books - Swan, Chalker, Quirk..

Have a look at these sentences then and tell me what you think.

1. Do not overtake cyclist's under the bridge.
2. You can tell a good language school by it's students.
3. The steerings OK.
4. I hope these photo's don't get ruined in the post.
5. The Private View will be opened formally by the acclaimed actress, Susan George, who's book of poems "Songs to Bedroom Walls" will be exhibited ...

6. Enjoy the best of both world's with a Summer cottage holiday.
7. Sign on window:

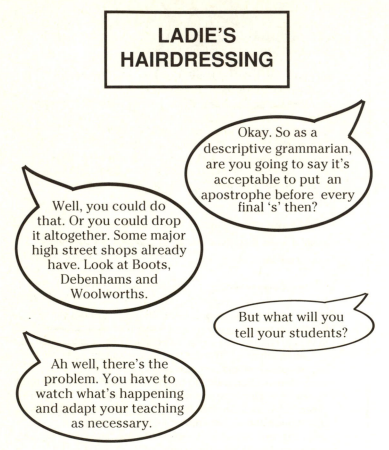

9.2 **What is your reaction to the above? Do you think your reactions are 'typical'? Compare them with other people's.**

Most of the above information was presented as a poster at the IATEFL conference in Warwick in April 1989. There was also a blank sheet attached to the poster for people to write their comments on. There was considerable interest in the problem, and some of the comments have been reproduced opposite.

`Insofar as punctuation is/contributes to a part of <u>meaning</u> it remains important to retain it. Examples of appropriate retention: people's vs peoples'; its vs it's. Where meaning is not in question the distinctions should be dropped - examples: dont, wont, cant vs don't, can't etc. With respect to the first comment above, <u>teaching</u> written language is dependent upon what we conceive written language to be. It is not a question of prescriptiveness, but precisely what we must be prescriptive about. It's time (not `its time'!) we all began to drop unnecessary apostrophes.'

`Have you tri'ed putting in ex'traneous ones? It woul'd cure any tendenci'es to g'o soft on this very real problem.'

`Or consult any greengrocer. (The major practitioner of error)'

`The prescriptive v. descriptive dichotomy was developed in relation to <u>spoken</u> language. It involves matters of language change and so on. Punctuation is a convention of written language. Written language is <u>taught</u> (even to native speakers) and so conventions are handed down - more or less effectively - to the next generation of writers by teachers. Hence teaching written language is prescriptive by definition. No linguist would argue that this is undesirable. Descriptive linguists describe language as it is, not as it should be (see Fries). That is not a problem in relation to your very interesting data.'

`Would you agree that, while a teacher has to be sensitive to changes in the language, he/she also has to act as a defender of correctness? Apostrophes are not just decorative, and if we were to get rid of them altogether, as you seem to be suggesting, the expressive power of the language will be diminished. If teachers do not defend standards, who else will?'

Adrian Room in an article in *English Today* cogently argues the case for abandoning the apostrophe. After outlining areas of English where it has already been dropped - for example, High Street shop names, many noticeboards naming Boys or Girls Schools, phrases like '*for goodness sake*' - he goes on to point out the advantages of dispensing with it altogether.

> First the ambiguities of spelling and usage ... would disappear. If we no longer write the apostrophe, we can never insert it incorrectly. Second, any initially odd-seeming spellings (*Jimll fix it, the actresss role*) would largely occur in colloquial English, but should soon be assimilated anyway. (Formal English would confine spellings of this type to the possessive.) Third, written English overall would be simpler, briefer and neater. Reported speech, which now contains a forest of quotation marks and apostrophes, would be considerably tidied up, avoiding sentences such as '*John's car's not there,*' *he'd said.*

9.3 **Is all this a storm in a teacup? Apparently not! The extracts opposite are from letters to the National press which appeared while this book was being edited. Do you agree with then? Why do you think the tiny apostrophe mark excites much comment?**

References
1. Road sign, Reading
2. Advertisement for a language school reported to me by a Danish teacher of English
3. Pitman Examination ESOL-403. 1989
4. The Oxford-Arels Preliminary Handbook, Greenhalgh, Pennington and Richardson. Edward Arnold 1988.
5. Invitation, Century Galleries, Henley, Oxon
6. Country Holidays brochure 1989 (1st edition)
7. Notice in the window of Sebastian's of Dorking

From Mr R A Walton

Sir: Since France has decided to kill its circumflex accent it might be an opportune time to retire our unpopular apostrophe, at least as far as its possessive use is concerned.

The personal pronouns (theirs, ours, hers) have never required it. Organisations have long abandoned it in registering their titles and top newspapers often use it inconsistently. And, while we are about it, we might as well forget it in such colloquialisms as "couldn't" and "don't". Punctuation, apart from the full-point and comma, has always been a nuisance. Surely it is high time that we continued with it only to clarify meaning rather than for mere decoration.

Sir: Mr R A Walton exhibits not only ignorance of the purpose of punctuation in general and the apostrophe in particular, but also of parts of speech (Letters, 15 July). Punctuation correctly used is never "mere decoration" but always has purpose; the apostrophe is not used with the pronouns "theirs", "ours" and "hers" because – like "its" – they are already possessive and require no punctuation to indicate this. Mr Walton's letter seems to advocate a further "dumbing-down" to meet declining literacy in a rapidly declining education system.

John Pye is correct that nouns may be used adjectively, as in his examples of sock shop and potato peeler. Similar uses are two-foot drop and ability test. The adjectival noun, however, is always used in the singular – never socks shop (although socks are sold in the plural) or two-feet drop. So if it is to be "schools test" (as opposed to school test) it must have an apostrophe.

Sir: Retire the apostrophe? How could greengrocers manage without them? We consumers rely on them for our potatoe's, tomatoe's and plum's.

My own apostrophic theory states that the number of apostrophes in the universe – or at least in Great Britain – is finite.

Thus the more misappropriated by greengrocers and florists (and recent university graduates), the fewer are available for proper use; whence such increasingly common malformations as "six years hard labour".

I have never claimed to be an apostrophe expert or even an apostrophes' expert, as John Pye opines.

....

The more recent *Grammar of Modern English* states: "It is becoming increasingly common nowadays in printed notices and headings to leave out the simple ' after a nominal ending in -s (eg boys school, ladies room)." The apostrophe is a moving target. I shall continue to hang on to it to express "appurtenance or association" and mourn its passing as I use the ladies' room.

CHAPTER TEN

WORD ORDER

The data so far has probably not been particularly surprising. You can walk down any High Street in Britain and find unusually placed apostrophes. The data about comparatives, conditionals and prepositions is frequent enough in my experience to be almost commonplace. There are, however, other areas where the data is less frequent and research reveals surprising information.

10.1 **Complete the sentences below by putting the words given in the correct order.**

1. You work out what ...
   your are benefit that ideas customers new the will

2. He asked ...
   engineer was the where

'He asked where was the engineer.'

3. I will never forget ...
   sister genius a your what was

4. They work out exactly how much ...
   every have giraffes day these should food

10.2 There are a number of possibilities, but see if you have come up with any of the sentences below.

1. You work out what are the new ideas that will benefit your customers.
2. He asked where was the engineer.
3. I will never forget what a genius was your sister.
4. They work out exactly how much food should these giraffes have every day.

Have a look at these examples too:

5. ...the public right to know how serious was the threat to their health.
6. He let his mind wander, wondering about her and Starke, about where were Erikki and Azadeh, about that Vietnam village ...

10.3 The question, therefore, is to what extent the word order above is acceptable in indirect questions. Decide how acceptable you think it is, then look at the information below.
First:

> When you report a question:
> * you do not treat it as a question by using interrogative word order

COBUILD (1990):

Then, this seems fairly categorical:

> Reported questions do not have the same word-order (auxiliary verb before subject) as direct questions often have.

Swan, Practical English Usage (1980)

But later he says

> In indirect questions, it is normal to put the subject before the verb.

The use of the word 'normal' is interesting there, suggesting that perhaps the inversion is retained in some situations which he is reluctant to go into at this level.

The fullest explanation is predictably from the major reference work:

> Although the subordinate clause does not have subject-operator inversion, such inversion may occur, particularly when the clause functions as complement and the superordinate verb is BE or when it functions as appositive

Quirk et al (1985)

and later:

> In literary style subject-verb inversion occasionally occurs when the wh-element is the subject complement, or an obligatory adverbial, particularly if the subject is lengthy.

I'm not sure that any of the sentences that I have collected are fully explained by Quirk et al. but at least they are prepared to admit the possibility of subject-verb inversion in an indirect question. The fact that their explanation of when this occurs is really quite difficult to understand and does not explain all of the examples that I have found suggests that it is not a distinction that we would want to teach students for the purposes of active production. However, the possibility of inversion does exist in indirect questions and it is something we should be aware of. It might also affect our classroom behaviour to some extent.

10.4 **How would you answer the questions below?**

    a. Would you mention the structure above to:

       (i) a class to whom you were presenting indirect questions for the first time?

       (ii) an advanced class with whom you were revising indirect questions?

    b. If a student asked you in class about one of the sentences above, what would you say?

    c. If an elementary student produced a structure similar to the ones above, how would you react?

    d. If an advanced student produced a structure similar to the ones above, how would you react?

References
1. Mark Brown. The Dinosaur. Element Books.
2. Gerald Seymour. Home Run. Fontana. 1989
3. ibidem
4. Informal conversation. 27.7.1990
5. BBC Radio 4. 8.2.1989
6. James Clavell. Whirlwind. Coronet 1986

In example 3 I swopped the word 'genius' for 'firechild' which was in the original. As 'firechild' is not given in the Shorter Oxford Dictionary I felt that it would make the exercise too difficult to leave it in.

CHAPTER ELEVEN

GERUND & INFINITIVE

The decision as to whether to use a gerund or an infinitive is one which is a constant source of heartache to many foreign students of English. Interestingly, there are examples of native speakers producing some very unusual sentences.

11.1 **Complete the following sentences with as many different structures as possible.**

1. Eventually I anticipate . . .
2. His back is toward you. But you could not reach him without . . .
3. Sybil the cat was not amused . . .
4. Ambulance services are shortly to refuse . . .
5. There's nothing legally we can do to make her . . .
6. We must . . .

11.2 **Did you come up with any structures like these?**

1. Eventually I anticipate to be almost as swift as your good self.
2. His back is toward you. But you could not reach him without he heard you.
3. Sybil the cat was not amused to be disturbed.

4. Ambulance services are shortly to refuse transporting more essential cases.
5. There's nothing legally we can do to make her to come home.
6. We must to watch out.

What do the reference books say about these structures?

The Oxford Advanced Learner's Dictionary admits to the possibility of number 3. But nothing else I have consulted allows for any of them - not COBUILD, not Swan, not even Quirk et al.

How then are we to deal with these sentences? The reference sources do not allow for them, they occur infrequently, and yet they have been produced by native speakers. What is more, in every case they are written examples - those that were spoken were all scripted.

At the risk of being inconclusive, my feeling is that we should just accept them as being interesting and possibly isolated instances. There is no law that states that everything we say or write has to conform to the rules grammarians have deduced from what has been said or written in the past. Nor is it necessary for future structures necessarily to conform to the examples above. They might be the start of a language change. They may just be a strange linguistic quirk that is unlikely to happen again. They may be attempts to express previously unexpressed concepts.

References
1. Jonathan Gash. Gold from Gemini. Arrow 1987.
2. Ronald Hardy. Wings Of The Wind. Wm Collins 1987
3. Spot. BBC2. (Children's television programme.) 24.10.1988
4. BBC1 News. 26.10.1989
5. BBC1. Eastenders. 24.1.1990
6. Mark Brown. The Dinosaur Strain. Element Books.

CHAPTER TWELVE

NUMBER

Another area of language that causes confusion, amongst students and sometimes native-speakers too, is number. There are problems with words such as *'fewer'* and *'less'* and problems with words which refer to groups and organisations.

12.1 Fewer/Less

'Fewer' and *'less'* is now a well-recognised area of language change. People with more hardened prescriptive attitudes, however, would not regard it as change and are frequently heard to lament the disappearance of *'fewer'*. But the fact remains that *'less'* is often used with countable nouns as well as uncountables.

How would you deal with these sentences if they were produced by a student?

1. There are less crews on the road.
2. You would have less cars on the roads and less accidents.

Swan (1980) writes 'in modern English a lot of people use *'less'* instead of *'fewer'* before plural words, especially in informal style. Some people consider this incorrect.'

Quirk et al (1985) have a similar comment and add 'This usage is . . . often condemned.'

Chalker (1984) says ' Careful speakers/writers make this distinction . . . There is however a growing tendency to use *less* (not *fewer*) for all nouns.' (Notice Chalker suggests the possibility for 'all' nouns.)

This use of *'less'* instead of *'fewer'* has therefore made its way into authoritative reference works. Chalker (1984) attaches no stigma to its use. She even suggests the possibility of using *'less'* with all nouns. Swan (1980) and Quirk et al (1985) both maintain a neutral status - for Swan some people obviously do not consider it incorrect; for Quirk et al it is not always condemned.

'This usage is often condemned'.

Swan also points out that it is common in informal style. Many teachers will be teaching their students a range of formality. Many students will be using their English in a spoken informal style. This usage is surely therefore one that students must be aware of.

Working on a draft of this text my editor drew my attention to a particularly fine example; early in 1989 the government's chief medical officer, asked about the danger of food poisoning caused by eggs, gave the memorable reply, *'Well, let's put it this way - less eggs would mean fewer cases of food poisoning'*. If we have a descriptive approach to language can we really condemn a usage that is so prevalent a part of spoken English?

12.2 Groups and Organisations

The interesting feature about words that refer to groups and organisations is their subject-verb agreement. This is not really a problem, but it is something which students in my experience find worrying. Students who are used to a black-and-white, right-or-wrong approach initially find it difficult to accept grey areas in language. The possibility that one word can be either singular or plural depending on how one looks at it is at first disturbing. Look at the sentences below:

3. A number of objections have been raised.

4. A quantity of drugs were seized.

5. Nationwide Anglia Fund Management announce their Rented Housing Business Expansion Scheme.

6. The British Insurance and Investment Brokers' Association has warned that car buyers should be wary of special car insurance deals.

7. The Red Cross has started work.

8. Harvey and Thomson, for example, charge 5 per cent interest per month.

9. Albermarle and Bond charge between 4 per cent and 6.75 per cent per month.

10. Tate & Lyle . . . is considering an offer for British Sugar.

Sentences 3 and 4 are illustrations of the well-established group of expressions which is (or are) followed by either a singular or a plural verb. Here we have 'a number' and 'a quantity' both of which appear to be singular and yet are followed by a plural verb. This group contains words such as *'family'*, *'team'*, *'government'*, *'orchestra'*, and many more.

Sentences 5 - 10 show how groups such as these, and named organisations, can either be seen as a totality or unit, i.e. singular, or separate individuals within a group, i.e. plural. There is no particular reason, as far as one knows, why The British Insurance and Investment Brokers' Association, The Red Cross, and Tate and Lyle wish to be seen as singular, whereas Nationwide Anglia Fund Management, Harvey and Thomson, and Albemarle and

Editor's Note: Readers may care to speculate on whether H.M. The Queen, delivering the Queen's Speech, setting out the Government's legislative programme for a session of Parliament refers to the British Government as *'My Government is keen to pursue . . .'* or *'My Government are keen to pursue . . .'* You will find the answer, at least for the Queen's Speech of October 1990 below.

Bond wish to be seen as plural. In the context in which these sentences arose - all from the same day's edition of 'The Independent' newspaper - the choice may well have been fairly arbitrary, the choice of the writer or sub-editor of each particular article or advertisement. That is not to say, however, that the choice is always unimportant. For a trade union, for example, it might be very important during, say, an industrial dispute to be seen as a single united body (*The union is demanding more money*) rather than a collection of individuals (*The union are demanding more money*). This is a point that we will return to later.

References
1. BBC1 News 13.9.89
2. A headmistress speaking on BBC Radio 4. 1990.
3. The Independent 8.9.90.
4. The Daily Telegraph. 7.6.89.
5 - 10. All the remaining examples are from the 8.9.90 edition of 'The Independent' newspaper.

Answer to Editor's Note (p58)
The reference is always *'My Government are . . .'*

CHAPTER THIRTEEN

OTHER POSSIBLE CHANGES

Apart from the examples previously given, observation reveals interesting data in other areas. In some of these there might even be a suggestion that a change in the language is taking place. The evidence to date, however, is slender.

We deal here with three areas:

Nationalities	(13.1)
Words	(13.2)
Other uses	(13.3)

13.1 Choose a word or phrase to complete each sentence:

1. A look at the work of .... architect, Lucien Kroll.
   (a) Belgian   **(b)** Belgium   **(c)** Belgium's

2. The Home Secretary has made an exclusion order against a ....
   (a) Northern Irishman   **(b)** Northern Ireland's man
   (c) Northern Ireland man

3. Can we take it the .... government is serious on this?
   (a) Iran   **(b)** Iran's   **(c)** Iranian

4. .... umpire Shakoor Rana made a controversial return to the international arena yesterday.
   (a) Pakistani   **(b)** Pakistan   **(c)** Pakistan's

Compare your answers with the key below:

1. b   **2. c**   **3. a**   **4. b**

This use of the country instead of the nationality is sometimes justified. During the 1990 World Cup football competition there was always reference to 'the Northern Ireland manager'. This was quite understandable since he was an Englishman. 'Northern Ireland' was the team he was managing. Similarly the players would be referred to as the 'Northern Ireland players' or the 'England team' not as a designation of nationality, which in the case of the players would be clear, but of the team they were representing. In the cases above, however, the country clearly stands as an indicator of nationality. None of the usual reference sources allow for this. It is something that is worth looking out for, and seems to be an increasingly common feature of contemporary British English.

References
1. The Independent 23.12.1989
2. BBC1 Nine O'Clock News 8.1.1990
3. BBC1 Six O'Clock News 11.4.1990
4. The Leader (a local newspaper) 1.9.90

13.2 **Choose which word (a, b or c) is least likely to complete the sentences below:**
1. 'In return for what?' Struan said, overwhelmed by the .... of the offer.
   (a) enormity   **(b)** size   **(c)** enormousness
2. What we can say will be .... and often controversial.
   (a) imprecise   **(b)** unprecise   **(c)** inexact
3. .... for your protection.
   (a) sanified   **(b)** sanitised   **(c)** sterilised
4. The .... of being the model son has never quite disappeared.
   (a) effort   **(b)** honour   **(c)** effortfulness

Compare your answers with the original sentences below:
1. 'In return for what?' Struan said, overwhelmed by the enormousness of the offer.
2. What we can say will be unprecise and often controversial.
3. Sanified for your protection.
4. The effortfulness of being the model son has never quite disappeared.

I consulted the dictionaries - the Oxford Advanced Learner's (OALDCE), the Longman Dictionary of Contemporary English (LDOCE), COBUILD, and the Shorter Oxford (SOED). *'Enormousness'* has a good pedigree and is recognised by OALDCE, LDOCE and SOED. *'Unprecise'* and *'sanified'* only come in SOED. And *'effortfulness'* is not given in any of the dictionaries.

I thought example 1 was unusual enough to arouse comment. Would you have corrected it in a student's work? Examples 2 and 3 both occur only in the two-volume Shorter Oxford Dictionary - hardly an essential reference work for students of English. What should the teacher's reaction be to a student producing 'unprecise' or 'sanified'? And finally what about 'effortfulness'? Is it 'wrong'? Can Anita Brookner be accused of 'not writing English'? But then, if she is allowed to twist the language and invent new words to serve her needs, so surely can more ordinary people, including non-native users of English. We do not deny scientists the right to invent words to describe new discoveries and concepts. Can one therefore deny any individual the right to invent words? The fact that they are not a scientist or a literary figure should be irrelevant. Creativity is surely something to be encouraged.*

In the modern world, there are also very large numbers of people who speak English as a second language. They, too, invent new words, according to their need to do so. It makes no sense to call these inventions 'mistakes'. On the contrary they are signs of highly sophisticated language use. It is important also to realise that this is not a skill confined to very advanced learners. Many teachers will have come across students at lower-intermediate level who have really tried to say what they mean even though they knew that they did not have the words to do it. They relied upon experimentation, unusual combinations of words, and sometimes just blind guessing, to see whether their attempt would communicate their meaning.

Editor's Note: Two facts to take into account, which work in opposite directions, are (a) is the word or phrase understandable? (b) is the user **consciously** choosing a non-standard form?

If language teachers take the view that language is either right or wrong, and that some words 'exist' or 'don't exist', they are going to inhibit these students, and destroy their creativity. In other words, this approach is going to make the students worse learners and worse users of English. That is, I feel, the opposite of what good language teaching is about. We need, therefore, to be flexible, and to encourage rather than discourage creativity.

I suggest we should not ask *'Does this word exist?'*, but instead we should ask *'Does this language express the speaker's or writer's ideas so that I can understand?'* If the language used does this successfully, then even lower-intermediate students should be encouraged to continue with a creative, experimental approach. In the long term, this will be to their benefit as language learners.

References
1. James Clavell. Tai-Pan. Michael Joseph 1966
2. F.R. Palmer. Semantics. CUP 1976, 1981.
3. Notice in bathroom, Redcar Hotel, Bath. 27.10.1988
4. Anita Brookner. Family and Friends. Cape 1985.

13.3 Study the sentences below. What is unusual in each case?
1. Sir Robin Day has ended his 20-year marriage in the London divorce court yesterday.
2. I'm owing you £2.20.
3. I'm needing this glass of water after that experience.
4. We've got a pile of letters which have been being typed since I don't know when.
5. By Vanbrugh's death in 1726 the West Wing was still unbuilt.
6. I've been to the British seaside last Sunday.

Comments
1. The present perfect is not normally used with past time markers such as *'yesterday'*.
2. The present simple would be more usual, describing the state of the speaker.
3. The present simple would be more usual for the same reason as in number 2.

4. The present perfect continuous passive is unusual.

5. The past perfect is more usual with expressions involving 'by a certain time in the past'.

6. The present perfect is not normally used with past time markers such as *'last Sunday'*.

Again, I would not wish to make too much of these rare instances. They do, however, demonstrate an important point - **speakers set out to create meaning**. They do this by **combining words and structures spontaneously to make their meaning clear**. They do not do it by constructing sentences on the basis of learnt (or learned) rules. English grammar, just as much as vocabulary, contributes to the meaning of what is said or written. If a speaker wishes to express a particular **meaning**, they* choose the grammar which helps them to do this.

The important thing is that language expresses the speaker's meaning, and is comprehensible. It is not a matter of applying rules. It is important to realise that native speakers speaking their own language never try to 'get it right', they try to say what they mean. It is only the foreign learner, doing an exercise for language learning purposes, who is 'trying to get it right'. That same learner, trying to use language for a real purpose outside the classroom, immediately stops worrying about getting it right and concentrates on communicating meaning. Hence the importance of 'communicative' approaches to language learning.

References
1. The Guardian 8.11.1985
2. Conversation in a supermarket 16.10.1987
3. The Beano. DCThomson and Co Ltd. 12.12.1987
4. Conversation with a colleague. 7.12.1988
5. Castle Howard brochure. Castle Howard Estate Ltd. 1988
6. BBC1. Paramount City. 19.5.1990

* Editors Note: The alert reader will have noticed that the author has just elegantly (and correctly!) referred to *'a speaker'* as *'they'*.

PART THREE

IMPLICATIONS

CHAPTER FOURTEEN

ACCEPTABILITY

14.1 One of the important points raised in Part Two is the idea of acceptability - what are we, as language teachers, looking for in terms of acceptability; how can we define acceptability; and how important is acceptability?

First we must decide what we are looking for in language terms when we talk of acceptability. What criteria are there, if any? From the standpoint of a language teacher, teaching students language that they will be expected to produce, we probably mean Standard English. It could be Standard British-English, Standard American, Standard Australian or even something like Standard Indian-English depending on the situation - but it will almost certainly be a Standard dialect. There may be special circumstances which require students to be taught a particular dialect, but they will be unusual. Students will be expected to understand a greater variety of language than they are capable of producing. It is expected nowadays that students will be exposed to a variety of dialects, accents and styles of English - so that they can understand them, but without necessarily being able to reproduce them.

The obvious corollary to this is that slang, while it might be considered acceptable within its own boundaries, falls outside the bounds of the acceptable Standard. That is not to say that we should dispense with or even get rid of slang. It serves a very useful purpose. It is very much part of a living language. It is a well of linguistic creativity. In some situations there will obviously be a need for students to be aware of, if not actually capable of producing, slang utterances. Certainly for those living in Britain or other English speaking countries it will be a necessary part of life.

Pronunciation

As far as pronunciation is concerned, greater latitude than ever before has become acceptable. Gone are the days when only Received Pronunciation (however it is defined) was the only acceptable accent for teaching purposes. Apparently Daniel Jones, the compiler of The English Pronouncing Dictionary, when asked how many people spoke RP, replied: ' Well, I do ... and my brother does ... but sometimes I'm not so sure about him.' As in the world outside the classroom, regional accents have at last become recognised as being of equal value to RP.

Education

Another favourite argument linked to the idea of acceptability is that of 'educatedness'. We very often talk about 'standard educated English', without, of course, defining 'educated'. We assume that it means 'having had some degree of higher education'. However, one could equally well argue that someone who left school at 16 with no formal qualifications, but reads Proust, Tolstoy and T.S.Eliot might also be described as 'educated'.

The concept of the 'educated' speaker is, however, linked to the idea of 'Standard English', where that is defined as the 'most widely comprehensible' form of the language. There are a number of reasons for this. Firstly, 'educated' people tend to be more mobile in their work. Teachers, for example, often seek promotion in a different part of the country or, indeed, in another country. Less educated people, on the other hand, are more likely to spend their working life in the same area. Secondly, the process of higher education forces the speaker of non-standard English to modify their language for greater intelligibility. Finally, education demands a degree of literacy which involves the ability to write standard English.

The so-called educated speaker, therefore, may use more than one code and be more aware of other codes than a person with no higher education. This suggests that such a person may have a concept of 'correctness' and 'acceptability'. They may also have a greater awareness of what language is 'likely' and 'unlikely'. In addition, and most important of all, they will probably also benefit from the greater articulacy necessary to use the language in any way they see fit in order to express their meaning as clearly as possible.

We must, however, be careful not to confuse the ideas of 'educated' and 'correct'. Most of the examples in this book were produced by 'educated' speakers of English. But many native speakers and non-native teachers would describe them as 'incorrect'. 'Educated' language use is neither superior nor inferior to any other form of English. Nor is the 'education' of the speaker necessarily any guide to the 'acceptability' of their remarks.

Medium

We must also consider medium. At its simplest this is the difference between written and spoken English. There are, however, deeper levels of complexity. Scripted news reports, for example, are spoken but perhaps reflect more the features of written English; whereas the script of a play is also written to be spoken but probably reflects more the features of spoken English. There is a tendency for unusual written examples to be dismissed as typesetting or proofreading errors. This cannot always be the case, especially where the example in question gets past author, editor, reader, typesetter and proofreader.

There is a similar tendency for unusual spoken examples to be dismissed as 'slips of the tongue'. This argument seems strange. We are at last beginning to get to grips with the differences between spoken and written texts. Discourse analysis is beginning to influence the teaching of spoken English. People are starting to realise that spoken English is very different from written English and that it does not necessarily function in the same way. We can no longer ignore this.

Frequency

The final factor that we will look at is frequency. A speaker or writer of Standard English produces an utterance or piece of text that is meaningful; it is not dialect or slang, yet it is not accounted for by the dictionary or grammar book. Is it acceptable? First let's have another look at some of the sentences we discussed in Part Two.

14.2 Read through the sentences below and decide if they are 'acceptable' or 'unacceptable'.

1. It was more clear than usual.

2. The Bradford City chairman has admitted that, in hindsight, there were other things that could have been done.

3. Have you an explanation of this?

4. Jack could hear him snoring very loud.

5. We wouldn't've met, if he hadn't've done it.

6. If it would be fun to do it, I would do it.

7. I hope these photo's don't get ruined in the post.

8. He asked where was the engineer.

9. Sybil the cat was not amused to be disturbed.

10. Can we take it the Iran government is serious on this?

How many did you mark unacceptable? If you marked more than one as unacceptable, you are beginning to tread on dangerous ground. With the exception of number 7, and possibly number 10, the rest can all be found in reference works somewhere. Even if they could not, it is still possible to argue that they are acceptable on the grounds that they were produced by native-speakers. As I have argued before, we **use** language and grammarians **describe** it. The language comes first, the descriptions follow. We do not have to fit our usage to grammarians' descriptions. Obviously it would make things easier for everyone if the language we produced always conformed to accepted grammatical descriptions. There would be no argument as to what is acceptable or not acceptable. But if we deviate, for whatever purposes, that does not invalidate the acceptability of what we have produced.

Finding unusual or 'deviant' utterances acceptable is obviously a very inconvenient position for language teachers. So let me propose again an alternative way of looking at things. Look at the ten sentences above again, and this time decide if you think they are 'likely', 'unlikely' or 'very unlikely'.

My guess is that this exercise is easier than the first. The only criterion is frequency - it is a **scale**, not an 'either - or' problem. It does not refer to arbitrary standards of 'education'. It is an objective judgement, not influenced by notions of style, historical acceptability or prejudice. It does mean that every utterance is 'acceptable' in the sense we have previously been using. But perhaps the idea of language being 'likely' or 'unlikely' provides a more useful perspective on these sentences and makes them easier to deal with. I shall examine this in more detail later.

CHAPTER FIFTEEN

LANGUAGE CHANGE

The data in Part Two suggests some definite areas of language change. Language is in a process of change - continuously and all around us. The fact that we are a part of it seems to make it that much more difficult for us to step back and view it objectively. Also our natural conservatism often tends to influence us into regarding new or unusual uses of language as 'lapses' or even 'mistakes' rather than genuine change. A brief look at some changes that have taken place in English over the past years should open up our minds to what might happen now and in the future. It will also demonstrate that there is no area of language that is immune from change.

Grammar

Take grammar first. Grammatical changes are easy enough to see over a longish time span. Many inflections that were once a normal part of the language have now been dropped altogether - *wilt* for *will*, *hast* for *have*, *shalt* for *shall* and so on. The second person forms *thou* and *ye* have disappeared except in a few dialects. The general trend seems to be towards the language losing inflections and becoming as far as possible an uninflected language.

And grammatical change is not just a phenomenon from the past. The subjunctive is still surviving despite considerable neglect. The uses of *may* and *might* when referring to past events have become confused and the two words are fast becoming regarded as synonyms. Finally, the distinction between *shall* and *will* may even be disappearing.

Pronunciation

Pronunciation too has changed. Since it is a feature of spoken language and therefore transitory by nature, it is perhaps not so easy to monitor. However, anyone who has seen old British newsreel or films from the early 1950s and before is certain to have remarked the difference between pronunciation then and now. The film 'Brief Encounter', made in 1946, is a wonderful demonstration of the short clipped vowels of that era where children are /frekshus/ (*fractious*) and people wear /hets/ (*hats*).

In addition, attitudes towards pronunciation have changed. Until recently it was frowned upon to speak with a regional accent. To many people it indicated a lack of 'education'. Almost all radio and television announcers spoke Received Pronunciation or 'Oxford English'. Nowadays, however, it is quite acceptable, fashionable even, to have a regional accent. When regional accents started to be used with greater frequency on radio and television, there was an immediate spate of letters of complaint. That though has died down, and it is now common and quite unremarkable to hear regional accents, even quite strong ones, on radio and television. Residual prejudices doubtless remain, but the initial barriers have been broken.

Punctuation

Even punctuation changes - an important point to remember when you think about the chapter on the apostrophe! Let us not forget that when writing started there was no punctuation at all - merely long lines of joined letters. Without going as far back as that though, this area is in a state of change, as much through the influence of word processors and related technology as anything else. Formal letters used to be indented at the beginning of every paragraph; now a line may be left between each paragraph instead. Organisations known by their initials used to be punctuated with a full stop between each letter - N.A.T.O., the B.B.C.; now they are NATO and the BBC. The acronyms went first, the rest followed. Philip Howard (1986) maintains that long sentences are gradually giving way to shorter sentences. Partly because the new technology copes with shorter sentences more easily. Partly because we do not have the patience any more to plough on to the end and work out what it all means. Probably also because it suits the style of the contemporary media to take short 'bites' of newsworthy texts to carry the essential message.

Words

Finally, of course, words change. The most famous example is probably *nice*. This word started its life meaning *'foolish'* or *'stupid'* in 1560. It went from there to *'wanton'* and *'lascivious'* in 1606. By 1769 it meant *'agreeable'* and *'delightful'*. And nowadays it is arguable whether it means anything at all! The original meaning of *prestigious* is 'practising juggling or legerdemain' - presumably it went from 'juggling objects' to 'juggling people or ideas' to its present meaning of *'influential'*.

There are one or two danger areas with words. A current bee in many people's bonnets is the growing use of *disinterested* to mean 'uninterested' rather than 'impartial'.

> Her mother had always been disinterested in her.

(COBUILD, 1987)

It is, people say, a sign of ignorance and an impoverishment of the language. The latter may well be true. However, the original meaning of *disinterested* was 'showing lack of interest' rather than 'showing impartiality'.

'Uninterested' or disinterested?'

Nor is word change confined to the distant past. A current trend sees the word *bad* going in a similar direction to *nice*. As a result of the influence of black American slang, something regarded as 'bad' no longer has connotations of evil, but is rather something to be admired. Other similar words have been affected in the same way as in: 'Did you see Michael Jackson on television last night? He was really wicked!'

Another change of meaning was recently brought about by the introduction of television cameras to the House of Commons. The new verb *'to doughnut'* is used to refer to Members of Parliament who sit around the person who is speaking so that they get themselves in the camera shot and therefore appear on television. Presumably when (if?) this practice ceases, so will the usage. Examples such as these have to be treated with care. Are they indications of real change or are they a transitory slang usage? Will 'bad' go the same way as 'fab', 'real', 'groovy', 'swinging', and 'far-out' - all of which have at some time meant good (or is it bad?) - and all of which have disappeared.

These are just a few of the different types of changes that have taken place over the years, and that are taking place now. It often appears that language change only took place in the past. The impression I often get from people is - *'Oh yes. A long time ago people used to say X and now we say Y. But what we say now is what is right and it's not going to change'.* They are prepared to admit that language **has** changed; but seem reluctant to acknowledge that it **is still changing**, that it will change more in the future, and that we are part of the process. There are other people who seem prepared to accept that language is changing now, but only in 'fringe' areas such as slang and colloquialisms. They are reluctant to believe that the change is more pervasive. The common core, they maintain, remains unaffected. I hope some of the examples quoted in this book worry them.

The language changes in the past are well accounted for. Perhaps some of the sentences in this book are the tip of a large iceberg for the future. Certainly they are all examples of contemporary language.

CHAPTER SIXTEEN

INVENTING NEW LANGUAGE

Chapter 13, while discussing other possible changes, raised the important point of invention. Native speakers are continually creating new words or using old words to create new meanings. We looked earlier at Anita Brookner's use of the word *'effortfulness'*. We have discussed how the meanings of some words have changed quite dramatically over the years. We have observed the fact that scientists are continually creating new words to label new inventions and discoveries.

However, this is not the prerogative of a privileged group of people. Most speakers of English quite frequently invent new words. Of course, if other people are going to understand newly invented words, the inventions obviously need to be systematic - to follow certain grammatical rules. Even if you have never met the word before, it is obvious what I mean if I say *'I am uncontactable for the next two weeks'*. The then Chancellor of the Exchequer, John Major, said on the main evening news (Sept 14 1990) *'We must go through this disinflationary phase'*. *'Disinflationary'* does not occur even in the Shorter Oxford Dictionary, but his audience knew what he meant. The question is not whether a word 'exists' or not, but whether, when it is used, it communicates the speaker's meaning to his or her audience. Very often if you want to say something original about an area you are not fully familiar with, you may need to invent a word. If this works, it must surely be perfectly acceptable.*

Editor's Note: Acceptable, yes. But we don't have to **like** some of these inventions. I recently heard, and took an immediate dislike to, the word *'de-installed'!*.

Humour too is often generated by word creation. Henry Widdowson at the Vienna Conference (1990) quoted the story of a radio programme in which the value of academic research was discussed. One of the participants mentioned a colleague he knew who had devoted a lifetime to researching ancient Greek hairpins. Within the context of the discussion this became the definitive example of 'indulging in academic enquiry with no contemporary relevance'. From that point in the discussion the word *'hairpin'* was used to refer to any similarly irrelevant academic pursuit. Another study was said to be an example of *hairpins*, or *a bit hairpinny* and so on. Obviously this form and meaning of the word 'hairpin' would not occur in any dictionary. And yet one cannot in any sense say that it is 'wrong'. All the participants knew exactly what it meant and, since it conformed to the 'rule' that inventions must be regular, they were all able to use it fluently and effectively.

An Aircraft carrier?

Similar linguistic phenomena happen within families and other close-knit groups of people. A long time ago my parents bought a garden table with benches attached - the sort one frequently finds in English pub gardens. My sister, aged about four at the time, realising that she did not have the language to deal with this new phenomenon called it an 'aircraft carrier'. And the term has stuck. We often still have lunch on the 'aircraft carrier'. We all know what we mean.

One of my sons, when aged three, invented a word of his own which loosely transcribes as 'ballywack'. This was a very useful word for him as it fulfilled the dual function of raising a laugh (often when trouble might be threatening) and standing in for any word which he did not know, or could not be bothered to think of! So successful was this ploy that, although it was recognised by his peers as his creation, they too took it up and it became part of the active linguistic repertoire of a small group of children in our area; and the passive repertoire of their parents!

These anecdotes also illustrate another basic premise that communication is achieved by the negotiation of meaning. Christopher Brumfit (1985) writes:

'What we in fact do (in any language) is **negotiate** our meaning by interacting and adjusting to the shared knowledge, the assumptions, even the linguistic ability, of the person we are talking to.'

And later:

'We need very little 'negotiation' to interpret *'Pass me a pencil, please,'* though even here we may need **some** 'negotiation', for we may interpret a *'pencil'* as 'something to write with' and pass a pen, which may provoke the reply *'Not that, a pencil'*, continuing the 'negotiation'. This is a personal and temporary example: *'pencil'* may not need to be distinguished from *'pen'* for the purposes of this interaction. But this illustrates our tolerance with meaning. We do not treat messages as if they have fixed, permanent, and rigid meanings. And as soon as we move on to more sophisticated examples , for example in philosophical or political discussion, or in legal disputes, or even in family arguments, it becomes clear that the same combinations of words may be extremely difficult to define, even within a specific context.'

Brumfit, Language and Literature Teaching: From Practice to Principle, Pergamon, 1985.

This is important. If we continue to accept the notion that language is something immutable, governed by rules, and which can be seen in terms of 'right' and 'wrong', we will be doing ourselves a disservice. It is not immutable; it is constantly changing and being twisted into new and different permutations. It is not governed by rules in the sense that rules dictate the way the language is used; 'rules' are derived from the way the language is used in the first place. And language use is dictated by the language user. Nor can language usefully be seen in terms of 'right' and 'wrong'. To do that is to impose an unrealistic straitjacket denying the language user the opportunity to play with and adapt the language, and to be creative.

As teachers we need to be constantly aware of this. How much of it we directly communicate to our students is something that we will look at in Chapter 18. What we must not do, however, is stifle students' creativity (or 'student creativity').

CHAPTER SEVENTEEN

THE POWER OF LANGUAGE

What interested me most about presenting some of the ideas in Part Two of this book as posters at IATEFL conferences was the strong reaction it aroused in many of the readers. Why should people feel so strongly about what is, after all, a perfectly natural process? Why do people get so upset at the fact that prepositions, for example, are not as predictable as some coursebooks and reference sources would like us to believe? I suspect that part of the answer lies in most people's strong reluctance to change. But part of the answer also lies in the close link between the control of language and the wielding of power. When people start to lose control over language, they begin to feel that they are in some way losing power.

This may seem a fanciful notion. But let us examine the idea more closely.

Malcolm X, at the inception of the Black Power movement, said *'Let us seize power. We are not negroes. We are blacks. Let us seize power.'* Why? Why is the idea of changing one's name from *'negroes'* to *'blacks'* in some way associated with seizing power? Because by getting rid of the name that the establishment had given them they were in some way getting rid of any power they felt the establishment had over them; and by themselves choosing what they should be called, they imbued themselves with a new power. On one level the change is symbolic; but the genesis of power is real.

As I write this (Autumn 1990), the Gulf conflict is well into its second month. So far, the battle has been one of words; seemingly a battle to decide whose account of the proceedings will prevail. Are the Westerners inside Kuwait and Iraq *'hostages'* or *'guests'*? Have the Western forces in

Saudi Arabia invaded the seat of Islam, as Saddam Hussein would have us believe, or are they there to defend Saudi Arabia from attack? Did Iraq *'invade'* Kuwait, or is its presence there *'in support of the popular uprising'?*

These battles of terminology are commonplace. In the early stages of US involvement in Vietnam, the anti-government forces were referred to as Viet Minh. This term, however, had been used to describe the resistance during the war of independence against the French and therefore had a strong, positive, freedom-fighting connotation. So the Americans invented the term Viet Cong, short for Vietnamese Communist, as a more negative, terrorist - oriented epithet.

'Communism' is a word fraught with danger. In many countries Communist parties are politically respectable. In other countries the term Communist is used to denote anyone who steps out of line with the government of the day. Any vaguely liberal-minded person would doubtless find themselves branded a communist in such a place. In the United States during the McCarthy years a supposedly democratic society allowed a witchhunt to take place resulting in social and political ostracism for those considered 'communist'. A recent news item in the British press reports that 'The Communist Party of Great Britain believes its name causes such loathing that it plans to reform under a new one.' Nina Temple, the party secretary, is quoted as saying 'The public perception of communism is of something entirely abhorrent.'

Further evidence of the power inherent in the name of a political party comes from the Liberal Democrat party in Britain. Formed from an alliance of the Liberal Party and the Social Democrat Party, they seemed to take an inordinate length of time agreeing on a suitable joint title. The public became bored with the whole exercise, jokes on the possible names abounded and the party lost some support during this period. But the people responsible, the politicians, were doubtless aware of how important the name could be.

The problems of naming do not stop with political parties. There are companies now whose sole function is to help their clients select names for new products. In part their function is to weed out names which, while acceptable in English, are totally unsuitable in another language. British Telecom apparently marketed an early portable telephone under the name *'tonto'*. Tonto is the name of the trusty Indian companion in the children's cowboy series 'The Lone Ranger'. It is also Spanish for *'stupid'*. Sales in Spain were presumably not good.

These firms are also responsible for discovering or creating new product names and researching the image that these names project. Calibra, the name of a Vauxhall car, is the creation of a company employed to develop a name for the new car and the result of extensive research.

Politics and marketing are not the only areas where language is used as an instrument of power. Almost all specialised groups of people have their own language identity. Lawyers, doctors, language teachers even, when talking shop, will often be almost incomprehensible to the lay person. With some groups it will be in their interest to maintain this mystique. It preserves their role in society. If we all knew what lawyers were talking about, we would probably pay them less, and might even dispense with them altogether. And this idea of language identity does not just apply to specialised groups. Gangs of children or criminals will develop their own slang to set them apart from their rivals. Pupils at British public schools often have a large 'alternative' slang vocabulary to learn in order to reinforce their identity as part of the group. The language we use therefore will in many respects reflect the groups we belong to.

Another aspect of the power of language is the uncomfortable and prevalent idea that the correct use of language can in some way be equated with education. As I have pointed out earlier there are problems with the argument which goes: this is what 'educated' people say, therefore it is 'correct'. The problem is one of defining what exactly 'educated' means. If we are to turn the argument on its head and suggest that 'educated people are those who speak correctly' we not only face the problem of what is 'correct' English, but also the fact that given the data collected in this book there cannot be many 'educated' people around. The argument becomes circular - which came first - the correct English or the education? Nonetheless, the idea of education is an important influence on people's attitudes. If we argue that 'correctness' is not a valid idea, that there are many language possibilities not accounted for by 'the authorities', it will be disturbing. People who feel they speak 'correct', 'educated' English will feel threatened. They will no longer be able to regard themselves as an elite.

So why do people become agitated when their accepted ideas about language are threatened? Is it just that they resent any change? This is a very common human trait. Or is it partly because they feel that a threat to 'their' language is a threat to them, their identity and their view of the world? As observers of language we must be aware of the influence that language has, the power it has over human behaviour, and the effect that any changes will have on the people who use it.

CHAPTER EIGHTEEN

IMPLICATIONS FOR TEACHERS

Obviously, being aware of language is vital for language teachers. We must also be aware of how language is really used rather than just how we are told it is used. The distinction between thinking of language in terms of likelihood rather than in terms of acceptability is also important. And while I feel these ideas have significant implications for language teachers, I am not proposing that they should immediately and radically change the way anyone teaches. What this approach should do, however, is raise teachers' awareness of some of the procedures they adopt in the classroom. It should lead them to reconsider some of the decisions they make on behalf of the students. And it could perhaps lead to greater dialogue between teachers and students about language in general and the language that is presented and practised in the classroom in particular.

18.1 **Let us look at some of the issues we raised in Part Two. Complete the following questionnaire:**

Which students, if any, would you make aware of the information below? Tick the appropriate columns.

	Elementary	Intermediate	Advanced	None
More' and 'most' are sometimes used with single syllable adjectives.				
Prepositional collocations are not fixed and unchangeable.				
The combination of verb forms possible in each half of conditional sentences is very large.				
The apostrophe does not always appear where you would expect it to.				
Word order in indirect questions is sometimes the same as in the corresponding direct question.				
The verb *'to refuse'* can be followed by an *'-ing'* form.				
The name of the country is sometimes used as an adjective rather than the nationality.				

If you have ticked any of the three left-hand columns, it would seem you agree that - to some extent - students should be made aware of the fact that the language people actually use is more varied than reference sources allow.

The main drawback of giving students this awareness is the uncertainty it arouses. Students, and often teachers too, feel happiest when issues can be seen in black and white, as right and wrong. When there is a murky grey area in the middle which is open to debate, people become uncomfortable.

The emphasis of much teaching today is on sharing with the students - not only sharing knowledge but sharing ideas, sharing feelings, sharing and negotiating the syllabus. I strongly agree with this emphasis. But it does pose an important question: To what extent can teachers share their **uncertainty** with students?

Like so much in teaching there is no single right answer. It will depend on the teacher and his or her style of teaching. It will depend on the students: their age - how some students will respond may depend on their age and maturity; their level - beginners might become confused by uncertainty, more advanced students may live with it more comfortably; their culture - teachers in some cultures may seem to lose 'face' or authority by confessing to uncertainty; their previous language learning experience - the nature and style of this may arouse certain expectations. It will also depend on whether students are in an English-speaking environment or not - those who are will quickly become aware that what they hear around them is not the same as what they are taught in the classroom. In addition there may be other local factors that will influence teachers in their decision as to whether to share uncertainties with their students.

An important point here is the selection of language. Obviously there is a 'core' of language which occurs with such frequency that its presence in any language course is not open to question. However, outside the 'core' there will be areas where someone has to make a decision as to what will or will not be included. In many cases the decision will in theory be taken by course designers, syllabus planners or other "higher" authorities. In practice though, it will often come down to the teacher in the classroom with a particular group of students. The factors listed above - age, level and culture - will also apply as much to what language selections the teacher makes as to whether the teacher confesses to any uncertainty. But in addition we will have to come back to the notion of frequency. How likely must a particular structure be to become included in your language teaching? Would you deal with the structure for recognition only? Would you deal with it for production? Oral production or written production? Or both?

There are other options open to us. We can deliberately avoid telling students certain facts. For example, we can omit to tell them that certain forms of conditionals are possible. That works until students find an example of one that does not fit what they have been told; or until they produce a perfectly correct utterance that has not been catered for by the teacher's explanation. Do you then correct it? Or do you ignore it and hope nobody else will notice?

The other possibility is to explain to students that what they are being told is not the whole truth but that for the moment it will suffice. Students are then aware that there is more to come on the subject; and, any correct but less likely language that arises at a later date will not be a total surprise. 'Rules', which often have to be incomprehensible in order to be true, can often be avoided in favour of 'hints' or 'guidelines' which can be easily understandable but not infallible. It is surely worth teachers taking time to explain the difference between 'rules' and 'hints/guidelines', and then making clear to students the status of any observation the teacher makes later. In addition, as students improve they can be presented with examples of the sort of material that we have been looking at in Part Two and asked to work out for themselves the processes that are going on in the language and how it is changing.

18.2 **Look again at the questionnaire on page 84 and for each of the points that you would share with students at a particular level, decide whether you would expect students to produce the language or only recognise it. And if they were expected to produce it, would it be for oral or written production, or both?**

Once you have decided how far you are going to allow grey areas of language to become part of your teaching repertoire, the very real problem of correction and marking arises. If, for example, students are aware that *'more'* can occur with one syllable adjectives, how will you deal with

students who produce this form? Can you in all honesty
mark it wrong? Or should you warn students it is correct
but unlikely? How would you deal with a student who
produces **only** *'more'* or *'most'* with one syllable adjectives?
Your actions will largely be dictated by the extent to which
you have decided to accommodate grey areas into your
teaching. But even if you have not informed students of
these grey areas, should they be penalised for producing
language that is possible, if unlikely?

18.3 **By way of an answer, look at these sentences from the
previous chapter and correct and annotate them as if
they had been produced by a student from one of your
classes.**

1. It was more clear than usual.
2. The Bradford City chairman has admitted that, in
   hindsight, there were other things that could have been
   done.
3. Have you an explanation of this?
4. Jack could hear him snoring very loud.
5. We wouldn't've met, if he hadn't've done it.
6. If it would be fun to do it, I would do it.
7. I hope these photo's don't get ruined in the post.
8. He asked where was the engineer.
9. Sybil the cat was not amused to be disturbed.
10. Can we take it the Iran government is serious on this?

Which sentences have you allowed to stand as correct?
Why?
Which sentences have you marked wrong? Why?

We make our own decisions about internal marking, but
not external. Can we guarantee that an external examiner
will share our own views on language and its acceptability?
The answer has to be no! Certainly we have a duty to teach
our students as well as we can and to the full extent of our
knowledge. But that surely includes the knowledge of what
the examiners are like and how best to pass the exam in
question. As teachers, most of us do things in class for the
sake of exams that we would not necessarily wish to do

otherwise. Telling students that certain structures and forms, while perfectly acceptable for everyday purposes, are best avoided in an exam, seems acceptable to me. An extension of the idea of register really, or analogous with learning to pass one's driving test rather than learning to drive.

So where does all this leave the reference books? Should we throw away the grammar and the dictionary and just rely on our own experience and intuition? Of course not! The reference books that I have quoted here are all well-used and invaluable sources of information. I would not be without them. What I hope to encourage is a more critical attitude towards them. They do not constitute 'the law'. They maintain that they are descriptions of the language. If what native speakers say or write does not fit with that description, you should not see it as the fault of the speaker or writer but a limitation of the dictionary or grammar. Record it or remember it. It might be unique and unrepeated; or it might be part of something more significant - a gradual change in current usage.

CHAPTER NINETEEN

REFERENCE BOOKS

Having quoted reference sources throughout this book, you will be entitled to ask which are reliable. This is a difficult question and one which I cannot fully answer. I can comment on the sources I favour but I cannot claim an all-extensive knowledge of grammars and dictionaries. I have written some comments below on the books which I find most useful. If, however, a book is not included in the list below, it does not necessarily mean that it is not useful, it may just be that I am not familiar with it. I have also included one or two books not mentioned so far but which are nonetheless useful as reference sources.

Grammars

A Comprehensive Grammar of the English Language. Quirk, Greenbaum, Leech & Svartvik. Longman. 1985.

For people who really want to get to the bottom of a grammatical problem this book is indispensable. It is by far the most thorough and wide-ranging of the grammars discussed here. Its 1,800 pages must contain all the grammatical information most people could possibly ever need to know - and despite its length and scope, it has an excellent index and cross-referencing system and is extremely easy to use. If you want something to help you prepare an explanation for your students, you will probably look elsewhere; but as an ultimate reference source this book is without parallel.

Practical English Usage. Swan. OUP. 1980.
I find this an extremely useful everyday reference source. It contains short explanations of a wide range of grammatical

points written in clear, easily comprehensible language. The explanations pay due attention to current grammatical thinking, and with its points organised in alphabetical order the book is extremely user-friendly. As well as teachers, advanced and upper-intermediate students find this book very useful.

Current English Grammar. Chalker. Macmillan. 1984
In my opinion this is a very underrated grammar. It is clearly organised and well-designed with each section containing summary boxes for quick reference. The explanations are up-to-date, concise and clear. This is also a book that advanced students would find useful.

Dictionaries

Oxford Advanced Learner's Dictionary. OUP. 1989.
Longman Dictionary of Contemporary English. 1978.
Collins Cobuild English Language Dictionary. 1987.
These are the main dictionaries I use for teaching purposes and for reference to do with language teaching. (At other times I use the two-volume Shorter Oxford English Dictionary, but that is rarely any help pedagogically.) The three listed above are all useful for students from upper-intermediate level upwards, and for teachers. There are a host of differences both major and minor between them. The Cobuild dictionary, for example, is 'based on a detailed of analysis of how today's English is really used'. The others are not. The Cobuild does not have illustrations. The others do. I find them all useful.

Longman Active Study Dictionary. Longman.
Oxford Student's Dictionary of Current English. 1988.
These two dictionaries are useful for students at elementary and intermediate level. I often find, when teaching, that it is a good idea to use a dictionary myself that is at the right level for the students I am teaching. So when teaching upper-intermediate or advanced classes, I will use one of the three in the section above. And when teaching elementary or lower-intermediate classes, I will use one of these two.

Other books

Brewer's Dictionary of Phrase and Fable. Cassell. 1959.

Known by its creator in 1870 as a 'Treasury of Literary bric-a-brac', and updated regularly since, this work contains a wealth of fascinating information. It aims to supplement the household dictionary and the general encyclopedia by providing information about and meanings of odd words and phrases. Or as Dr Brewer himself said, to give 'the Derivation, Source, or Origin of Common Phrases, Allusions, and Words that have a Tale to Tell.' Where else would you find out the qualifications necessary for a man to be addressed as 'esquire', the origin of the phrase 'a bit of fluff', the meaning of 'the Chiltern Hundreds'? This is not an essential book for language teachers; but it is for language enthusiasts.

Oxford Dictionary of Current Idiomatic English. OUP. 1975 & 1983.

A very useful two-volume reference source for idioms and phrasal/prepositional verbs. Although a standard dictionary will usually provide most of the information you might need, specialist dictionaries for idioms or phrasal verbs are sometimes useful when more than the basics are required.

Everyman's English Pronouncing Dictionary. Jones. Dent. 1967.

As with idioms, standard dictionaries are good adequate sources of information for pronunciation. However, if I want to appeal to the highest authority, I will turn to a good pronouncing dictionary such as the one above. At random, while writing this, I looked up the word *'handkerchief'*. The Oxford Advanced Learner's gives two different pronunciations; Cobuild gives one - the same as one of the Oxford ones; the Longman Dictionary of Contemporary gives one pronunciation that is the same as Oxford and Cobuild, and one that is different from either of them. In all a total of three possible pronunciations, and no dictionary gives all three. Except the pronouncing dictionary.

CHAPTER TWENTY

DATA COLLECTION

It is an interesting and worthwhile exercise to record unusual phrases that you come across. Once you start to record data then patterns begin to emerge, and the frequency or infrequency of occurrence will help you decide how important different observations are.

As I pointed out in the Introduction, I have used no special language corpus for the writing of this book. Living in England provides an adequate exposure to the language. For people living in a non-English-speaking environment it will obviously require more effort. However, as long as you have access to current English the opportunity is there.

As for how to keep a record of your data, one or two different methods are possible. Someone* I know tears the relevant piece out of the newspaper (I do not know what they do with books!), records the date and publication on the piece of paper and keeps all the pieces in a trunk in their flat. The advantage of this is that they have the authentic piece of paper and often the whole text; the disadvantages are that there is no systematic record and that retrieval is difficult. It also takes no account of the spoken word.

I keep all my data in a school exercise book. I record the phrase itself - and as much of the surrounding language as is necessary. I also note the date and the situation (or radio/television programme) if it is a spoken item; the publication, author, publisher and copyright date if it is written. I number the pages of the exercise book. And I

* **EDITOR'S NOTE:** I admit it! (Incidentally, *I do* record spoken examples, and I have endless photocopies of odd pages of books! My own observations endorse every line the author suggests in this book!

keep an index in the front of the book where I list each entry by page number in whatever category I think it best fits. So the front of the book looks something like this:

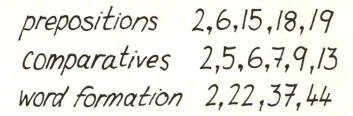

prepositions 2,6,15,18,19
comparatives 2,5,6,7,9,13
word formation 2,22,37,44

and so on. This allows me to monitor frequency easily and to find particular items quickly.

Generally speaking, I do not note items straight into the exercise book. Having collected all this data over the last five years, one of my greatest fears has been losing it all! I keep the book safe at home and record the item on whatever scrap of paper comes to hand. When I have half a dozen scraps together I transcribe them all into the book at the same time.

I am sure other people, especially the computer literate, will invent, or even already have, their own perfectly acceptable alternative systems. But if you have not yet started, this one does work reasonably well.

Not living in an English-speaking environment can, as I have remarked above, make data collection more difficult. There are, however, ways of tackling this. First, access to English films and television programmes is far more widespread than it used to be. English newspapers are also readily available in most countries. If your exposure to English is limited, you should probably try and make more of the little that there is. For example, whereas I will usually read the newspaper for pleasure, concentrating only on the articles that interest me, and find one or two unusual phrases a week or even a fortnight; it might be worth going carefully through the paper, or even just one page of the paper, deliberately looking for material that you find odd.

I had already read the day's newspaper for pleasure, and did not find anything worthy of note. But when I looked through it again more carefully, I discovered a wealth of interesting language.

The following phrases and sentences all came from just three pages of The Independent (12.9.1990):

1. After Mr Ryzhkov had outlined to Soviet MPs a redraft of his spring plans ...

2. Mr Shatalin, however, declined to outline his ideas to the Soviet assembly ...

3. Mr Gorbachev's new spokesman, Vitaly Ignatenko, said they should not be working in the Soviet Union if they could not take a little confusion.

4. If you free prices, only God knows what will happen.

5. If you've been tuning into Channel 4 between 9.25 and 11am, you will have seen one of the most appreciated programmes on TV.

6. Their 6.4m of paid advertising outspent Labour by almost three to one in 1987.

7. National Magazines and Conde Nast will be fighting on a second front next spring when Conde Nast's Vanity Fair will be published in London ...

8. That's very encouraging to me.

9. I made the mistake of ignoring that Leeds were a British team.

Numbers 1 and 2 show two different patterns from the same article used with the verb to *'outline'*. None of the dictionaries I consulted account for this.

Numbers 3, 4 and 5 are all examples of conditionals which fall outside the scope of the traditional first-second-third categories. In Number 3 the problem is compounded in that the condition is reported - nonetheless there are modals in both parts and not a *'will'* or a *'would'* in sight. Number 4 has present simple in each part - a common occurrence sometimes taught as the 'zero' conditional. Number 5 has present perfect in the *if*-clause and *will* with a past infinitive (sometimes known as the future perfect) in the main clause.

Number 6 contains the verb to *'outspend'*. This does not occur in any learner's dictionary (learners' dictionary? – I'm not sure which the author intends! Ed.), though it does appear in the Shorter Oxford. It would appear therefore to be an uncommon word. Its meaning is easily deducible.

Number 7 contains an interesting use of *'will'* in a *'when'* clause. This contravenes what one recent grammar says 'if the time clause refers to something that will happen or exist in the future, you use the **simple present tense**, not a future tense.'

Number 8 is an interesting prepositional use, unaccounted for by the dictionaries. It makes perfectly good sense, but is a little unusual.

Number 9 gives a very unusual sentence pattern after the verb *to ignore*. Again unaccounted for by any of the reference sources.

So... quite a rich haul for twenty minutes work reading three pages of the newspaper carefully. Awareness of what people really say and write requires no particular skill, merely a little extra alertness. A small investment of time spent on observation may produce some surprising results.

CHAPTER TWENTY ONE

EXAMPLES FOR DISCUSSION

All the extracts in this chapter are for your consideration. Each extract comes from a piece of standard English writing or speech. Each extract contains at least one example of English which may cause you to raise an eyebrow, or may cause your students to question a particular usage. Some are further illustrations of problems discussed earlier in this book; others are completely different.

I suggest you follow the procedure below:

a. Observe the usage.

b. Compare what different reference books say about the point.

c. Discuss it with as many colleagues or native speaker friends as you can.

d. Keep a lookout for more similar examples.

If you have difficulty deciding what point you should be considering, consult the key at the end of the chapter.

1. We will then have the option to producing a third level.

2. New Zealand's pacifism had rendered it unable of deciding a policy on the Gulf crisis.

3. Mrs Thatcher was careful not to talk up the prospect of war.

4. You might just better check with the Principal.

5. You had many enquiries on it?

6. We support our accountants's costings.

7. I just sip away all day and wonder what could have been had had I have had George's talent in my own field.

8. If I did anything to change that, I'm proud of it.

9. You should take no action on this letter.

10. Improving Oxfords Council Housing.

11. In future we are going to know how effective is the treatment.

12. In future we are going to know how much does it cost.

13. Both British girls don't make the final.

14. All of the main credit cards are not allowed in the store.

15. The removal firm Pickford's are collecting tents and clothings for the victims.

16. *Customer's*

    Due to staff shortage this door is temporally closed.

17. Topics which have been or will be offered in the past include the Communicative Testing of English ...

18. The pretty office girl came in and handed to Morse a buff-coloured file.

19. We have not done such an inquiry here.

20. If companies genuinely believe in the short-termist concerns they express, they should clearly do all they can to improve matters by their own actions.

21. It looks as if there will be a national championships in 1991.

22. If the city has things right, Clare Enders has the hardest job in television.

23. Everybody must be very glad on that.

24. This footpath is not a public highway and it's use is with the consent of Reading Borough Council.

25. ...hopelessly equipped companies turning out shoddy goods that no one would buy for choice.

References

1. Personal correspondence - 7.9.90

2. The Independent. 21.8.90

3. The Independent. 22.8.90

4. Conversation - 20.7.90

5. Conversation - 19.9.90
6. Memo - 6.8.90
7. Jeffrey Bernard on George Best. The Independent on Sunday. 23.9.90
8. The Independent on Sunday. 30.9.90
9. Wiggins Teape Appleton circular. 27.9.90
10. Hoarding, Oxpens Road, Oxford. 4.10.90
11. Kenneth Clarke. BBC Radio 4. 9.10.90
12. Kenneth Clarke. BBC Radio 4. 9.10.90
13. BBC Grandstand. 26.10.1985.
14. BBC Radio 4. 8.5.1989.
15. ITN News. 24.9.1985.
16. NSS Newsagents, Caversham. 15.11.1987.
17. English Language Training courses brochure, IELE, University of Lancaster 1988.
18. Colin Dexter. Last Seen Wearing. Pan Books. 1977.
19. BBC1. Nine O'Clock News. 15.5.1990.
20. The Independent. 25.10.90
21. The Independent. 24.10.90
22. The Independent. 24.10.90
23. Douglas Hurd quoted in The Independent. 23.10.90
24. Council notice. 20.7.90
25. The Independent. 14.7.90

Key

1. *'Produce'* or *'producing'.*
2. *'Of'*?
3. Is *'to talk up'* a new phrasal verb?
4. *'Might just better'*?
5. I would expect *'about'* rather than *'on'.*
6. The apostrophe!
7. An extra *'have'* in the conditional?
8. Interesting tenses in the conditional.
9. *'On'*?

10. A missing apostrophe?

11. Look at the word order.

12. Look at the word order.

13. *'Both ... not'* usually = *'neither'.*

14. *'All ... not'* usually = *'none'.*

15. *'Clothings'*?

16. The apostrophe. And presumably *'temporarily'* was intended rather than *'temporally'*!

17. *'Will'* in the past?

18. Or is *'handed Morse a buff-coloured file'* more usual?

19. Do you usually *'do'* or *'make'* an enquiry?

20. A new word?

21. Is *'championships'* singular or plural?

22. Look at the tenses in the conditional.

23. *'On'*?

24. The apostrophe. Again!

25. *'For'*?

Here is a final set of up-to-date examples, this time without any comments. All of them are real examples that I have recorded while writing this book. If possible, discuss them with your friends. See what your grammar reference books say. How do you feel about them? Do they influence your view of English any way? How about your view of *teaching* English?

1. Far more filmic than literary really.

2. In such a circuit it is suggested to include a pair of crossover tracks to equalise the distances travelled.

3. . . . acting in a more choiceful way . . .

4. I'm interested to know more about . . .

5. At no cost to you and with no charge to your students.

6. If you want a simple cut try a barbers.

7. They have threatened to revenge his death.

8. Has any of your readers noticed . . .

9. I wonder if any of your readers have noticed . . .

10. She's been in two weeks ago.

11. Who shall save Thatcherism?
12. Simply because we're getting more cases done.
13. Mr Yeltsin appeared shoulder to shoulder with Mr Gorbachev on Red Square.
14. The progressivists are not done yet.
15. Just how high are the stakes is illustrated by George Younger.
16. If the collectors panel hasn't arrived, roads/streets should be booked in advance.
17. Anne Wiseman is particularly interested in developing ideas for teachers who work with little resources.
18. It's a lot more safe.
19. That's one area where we are wanting it.
20. They still did not understand what was the basis of the case.
21. Saddam Hussein doesn't realise how great is the danger of war.
22. It takes place in Christmas.
23. There is a detestable aroma of snobbism and elitism.
24. If he'd've driven on, he'd still be alive.
25. One is sickened by touristic pollution.
26. I have yesterday inspired Crystal to send out letters.
27. The audience assembles for a performance last night . . .
28. Many Tory MPs are wondering what on earth they've done in getting rid of her.
29. Then why so little results?
30. Not Mrs Thatcher but one of her most staunch and pugnacious supporters in the Press.
31. That comes relatively little into syllabus design.
32. . . . . clear ability at making a speech.
33. . . . immense ravines, visited by an infinitude of darting swifts and swallows.
34. . . . where we had previously been treated with morose indifferentism.
35. Morrells – Oxfords Only Brewery.
36. I think I've got a more deep understanding of politics.
37. The economic situation is very, very desperate.
38. Continue baking until the cake has shrunken slightly from the sides of the tin.

References

1. John Berger. The Independent. 26.10.90
2. 27 Circuits for Scalextric. Hornby Hobbies Ltd. 26.10.90
3. Professional lecture. 27.10.90
4. Conversation. 27.10.90
5. Letter from One55 (an EFL student magazine). 11.9.90
6. One55 (pilot edition). 29.10.90
7. BBC1. 9 O'Clock News. 6.11.90
8. Letter to Private Eye. 9.11.90
9. Letter to Private Eye. 9.11.90
10. Private conservation. 10.11.90
11. Mail on Sunday. 11.11.90
12. The Independent Magazine. 10.11.90
13. BBC1. 9 O'Clock News. 13.11.90
14. Today. Radio 4. 13.11.90
15. Radio 4. News report. 14.1.90
16. ActionAid. Plans for Co-ordinators for House to House Collections. June 1st - 15th 1991.
17. Practical English Teaching. September 1990.
18. Conversation. 14.11.90
19. Oxford Teacher's Club talk. 15.11.90
20. Letter. 8.11.90
21. BBC1. 9 O'Clock News. 10.11.90
22. Omnibus. BBC1. 15.11.90
23. Steven Berkoff. Letter to The Independent. 17.11.90
24. An Unkindness of Ravens. Ruth Rendall. ITV. 18.11.90
25. Anthony Burgess. The Independent. 11.1.91
26. Meeting. 20.11.90
27. Today. Radio 4. 21.11.90
28. Newsnight. BBC 2. 21.11.90
29. Die Kinder. BBC 1. 21.11.90
30. The Independent Magazine. 24.11.90
31. Talk at ARELS-FELCO conference. 24.11.90
32. Radio 4. 28.11.90
33. Howard Jacobson. In The Land Of Oz. Penguin 1988
34. Howard Jacobson. In The Land Of Oz. Penguin 1988
35. Sign. The Westgate Pub. Oxford. 28.11.90
36. Radio 4. 28.11.90
37. Today. Radio 4. 29.11.90
38. The Neff Recipe Collection. 5.12.90

CHAPTER TWENTY TWO

POSTSCRIPT

Some time ago I wrote a memo at school in which I suggested that some of the optional subjects taught might be *'sidelined'* or *'retimetabled'*. One of my colleagues remarked on the use of *'sidelined'* as a verb, suggesting that this was 'incorrect'. In fact *'sideline'* is listed as a verb in the Shorter Oxford Dictionary, but only with the meaning of to 'hobble an animal'. Had I created a new use? I doubted it. Within a short time I had come across these examples:

1. This was big enough for the investigation of which Harlech was Case Officer to be sidelined ...

2. Less than two months ago surgery on the same knee sidelined him for three weeks.

3. The Zulus fear they will be sidelined.

4. He missed an opportunity for a final crack at the England captain, Graham Gooch, who was sidelined with a finger injury.

Obviously there were other people who thought that *'sideline'* could be used as a verb with the meaning of to 'put someone or something to one side.' Language use had again outpaced the dictionary.

Interestingly the use of *'timetable'* as a verb, which was not commented upon, is not listed in the Shorter Oxford Dictionary either. Though it is given in the Cobuild English Language Dictionary and the Longman Dictionary of Contemporary English. Another new use perhaps?

This incident emphasises the main thrust of my argument throughout this book. Language awareness is all important. Grammars, dictionaries, lexicons, other reference sources are useful. But there is no substitute for the observation of 'real' language. 'Real' language being what people say or write, not what the 'authorities' tell us we should say or write. Such observation will show us the full range of language possibilities. It will help us monitor language change in action. And it will, I hope, demonstrate that, from an observer's point of view, language is better seen in terms of 'likely' and 'unlikely' rather than 'right' and 'wrong'.

As teachers we may not wish to share all our uncertainties with our students. However, greater awareness of 'real' language will, I hope, begin to exert an influence on both what we teach and how we teach it.

References
1. Gerald Seymour. Home Run. BVHolland Copyright Corporation 1989.
2. The Independent. 17.7.90
3. The Independent. 14.10.90
4. The Independent. 25.10.90

BIBLIOGRAPHY

Allsop, J. Cassell's Students' English Grammar. Cassell 1983.
Brumfit, C. Language and Literature Teaching: From Practice to Principle. Pergamon. 1985.
Chalker, S. Current English Grammar. Macmillan 1984.
Close, R.A. English as a Foreign Language. Allen and Unwin. 1962.
Collins Cobuild English Language Dictionary. Collins 1987.
Collins Cobuild English Grammar. Collins 1990.
English Language Teaching Journal. OUP.
English Today. CUP.
Fowler, H.W. & F.G.Fowler, The King's English. OUP 1982.
Howard, Philip. The State of the Language. Penguin 1986.
Lewis, M. The English Verb. LTP. 1986.
Longman Dictionary of Contemporary English. Longman 1978.
Oxford Advanced Learner's Dictionary of Current English. OUP 1989.
Oxford Student's Dictionary of Current English. OUP 1988.
Partridge, Eric. Usage and Abusage. Penguin 1975.
Practical English Teaching. Mary Glasgow Publications.
Quirk, R & S. Greenbaum, G. Leech, J. Svartvik. A Comprehensive Grammar of the English Language. Longman 1985.
Quirk, R & S. Greenbaum, G. Leech, J. Svartvik. A Grammar of Contemporary English. Longman 1972.
Shorter Oxford English Dictionary. OUP 1973.
Swan, M. Practical English Usage. OUP 1980.
Swan, M & C. Walter. Cambridge English Course. CUP. 1984.
Widdowson, H. Proper Words in Proper Places. Paper, Vienna Conference 1989.